Praise for *The Seco...*

T0009341

"Every couple needs to read *The Second Happy*. We've often said that marriage doesn't make you happy, you make your marriage happy. And it's a sentiment that Kevin and Marcia live out in their own relationship. Now, in this engaging book, they let us in on their secrets. You don't want to miss out on their message. It's easy to grasp and put into practice. Most importantly, it works."

—Drs. Les and Leslie Parrott, #1 *New York Times* bestselling authors of *Saving Your Marriage Before It Starts*

"Marriage can be awesome and God-honoring, but it never gets there by accident. It takes intentional effort to counteract the things that steal joy, shut down communication, or leave you stuck in a cycle of unending disappointment. If you've been hoping for more but settling for less, Kevin and Marcia's new book *The Second Happy* can give you the tools to do something about it. I know this couple. They live what they teach, and their practical and inspirational wisdom can help you take your marriage to the place you've always hoped it could go."

—Craig Groeschel, pastor of Life.Church and *New York Times* bestselling author

"Wouldn't it be great if marriages came with a road map? A trusty guidebook for navigating the ups and downs of wedded bliss? Well, with their book *The Second Happy*, Kevin and Marcia Myers have created a road map of seven practices that will turn your marriage *vows* into marriage *values*—lasting principles to help you build the married life of your dreams. I know Margaret and I would have benefited from this book early in our marriage. But the beautiful thing is, you don't have to be newly wed or oldly weary to learn from this book! The advice is timeless, and so are the benefits of reading *The Second Happy*."

—John C. Maxwell, *New York Times* bestselling author

"Kevin and Marcia Myers have a gift for helping married couples grow closer in their relationships, with each other and with God. *The Second Happy* offers first-rate wisdom sure to revive, recharge, and renew the love anchoring every marriage. Told with honesty, humor, and humility, this book is the perfect wedding present couples can give themselves."

—Chris Hodges, senior pastor of Church of the Highlands and author of *The Daniel Dilemma* and *Out of the Cave*

"In *The Second Happy*, my dear friends Kevin and Marcia share marriage wisdom that is unique, pragmatic, and biblical. Rather than searching for a way out of your marriage, let them help you find practical ways to engage with your spouse. After forty-two years of marriage myself, I can promise you that conflict will never go away. But you can learn from Kevin and Marcia the art of compromise for a happy marriage!"

—Sam Chand, leadership consultant and author of *Harnessing the Power of Tension*

"I was there when these two 'kids' were married nearly four decades ago! Different in personality and background, they each had a commitment to grow personally and a common desire to grow together, not apart. The result of their relational investment is not only being happy now but healthy in a way that extends to their family for generations to come. The lessons they learned are shared with transparency and humor in this book that benefits us all!"

—Wayne Schmidt, general superintendent of the Wesleyan Church

the second happy

the
second
happy

SEVEN PRACTICES TO MAKE YOUR MARRIAGE
BETTER THAN YOUR HONEYMOON

Kevin & Marcia Myers

WITH CHARLIE WETZEL

NELSON
BOOKS
An Imprint of Thomas Nelson

The Second Happy

© 2021, 2022 Leadership Gravity, LLC, and Wetzel & Wetzel, LLC

All rights reserved. No portion of this book may be reproduced, stored in a retrieval system, or transmitted in any form or by any means—electronic, mechanical, photocopy, recording, scanning, or other—except for brief quotations in critical reviews or articles, without the prior written permission of the publisher.

Published in Nashville, Tennessee, by Nelson Books, an imprint of Thomas Nelson. Nelson Books and Thomas Nelson are registered trademarks of HarperCollins Christian Publishing, Inc.

Published in association with Yates & Yates, www.yates2.com.

Thomas Nelson titles may be purchased in bulk for educational, business, fundraising, or sales promotional use. For information, please e-mail SpecialMarkets@ThomasNelson.com.

Unless otherwise noted, Scripture quotations taken from The Holy Bible, New International Version®, NIV®. Copyright © 1973, 1978, 1984, 2011 by Biblica, Inc.® Used by permission of Zondervan. All rights reserved worldwide. www.Zondervan.com. The "NIV" and "New International Version" are trademarks registered in the United States Patent and Trademark Office by Biblica, Inc.®

Scripture quotations marked ESV are taken from the ESV® Bible (The Holy Bible, English Standard Version®). Copyright © 2001 by Crossway, a publishing ministry of Good News Publishers. Used by permission. All rights reserved.

Scripture quotations marked GNT are taken from the Good News Translation in Today's English Version—Second Edition. Copyright 1992 American Bible Society. Used by permission.

Scripture quotations marked THE MESSAGE are taken from *THE MESSAGE*. Copyright © 1993, 2002, 2018 by Eugene H. Peterson. Used by permission of NavPress. All rights reserved. Represented by Tyndale House Publishers, Inc.

Any internet addresses, phone numbers, or company or product information printed in this book are offered as a resource and are not intended in any way to be or to imply an endorsement by Thomas Nelson, nor does Thomas Nelson vouch for the existence, content, or services of these sites, phone numbers, companies, or products beyond the life of this book.

ISBN: 978-1-4002-0852-4 (TP)
ISBN: 978-1-4002-0851-7 (audiobook)

Library of Congress Cataloging-in-Publication Data

Names: Myers, Kevin, 1961- author. | Myers, Marcia, 1962- author. | Wetzel, Charlie, 1960- author.

Title: The second happy: seven practices to make your marriage better than your honeymoon / Kevin and Marcia Myers with Charlie Wetzel.

Description: Nashville: Thomas Nelson, 2021. | Includes bibliographical references. | Summary: "The Second Happy is a captivating, practical resource that provides the tools necessary to tune-up, overhaul, or even rebuild your marriage. Practices to sustain and strengthen marriage include the following: breaking the quit cycle; picking a fair fight so both people win; keeping disagreements from escalating; and removing pretense from your relationship. Rooted in Scripture and contemporary insights from the Myers' marriage, as well as real stories from other couples, this revelatory book shows how any marriage can regain depth, meaning, and, yes, happiness"—Provided by publisher.

Identifiers: LCCN 2020027624 (print) | LCCN 2020027625 (ebook) | ISBN 9781400208494 (hc) | ISBN 9781400208500 (epub)

Subjects: LCSH: Marriage—Religious aspects—Christianity.

Classification: LCC BV835 .M955 2021 (print) | LCC BV835 (ebook) | DDC 228.8/44—dc23

LC record available at https://lccn.loc.gov/2020027624

LC ebook record available at https://lccn.loc.gov/2020027625

Printed in the United States of America

22 23 24 25 26 LSC 10 9 8 7 6 5 4 3 2 1

To Joshua, Julisa, Jake, and Jadon.
You are four of God's greatest gifts to us.
We love being your parents and are so very proud of you.
Mom & Dad

Contents

Introduction 1

Practice 1: Break the Quit Cycle 9

Practice 2: Get Your Hands Up 41

Practice 3: Pick a Fair Fight 71

Practice 4: Take a Knee or Two 101

Practice 5: Don't Settle for the Hollow Easter Bunny 129

Practice 6: Evict the Elephant 163

Practice 7: Choose Your Bucket Wisely 195

Conclusion 221

Acknowledgments 223

Notes 225

About the Authors 227

Introduction

Everyone wants a happy marriage. And nearly all marriages start out happy. Our marriage was no different. It started out happy as we enjoyed a honeymoon season, but it didn't take long to lose a lot of that happiness. We think that's pretty typical of marriages—or at least 99 percent of them. If you're in the 1 percent, then give this book to a friend. Now, where were we? Oh, yeah.

For most of us, we become less happy with our marriage as time goes along. It's a lot like the way most of us feel about our houses after some time has passed. For example, when our kids were young, we became unhappy with the house we were living in, so Marcia and I went searching for a new one, specifically one with a big front yard for the kids. We found it, and we loved it—for a while. But the truth was that the master bathroom was small. I mean really small. The forty-two-square-foot space (it was seven feet by six feet) included a toilet, a shower, a sink, and a linen closet. We accepted that cramped footprint at first, but over time we became less happy with it.

What did we do? We sold it and moved into a new house. We were so happy. But after living there for a decade or so, parts of it became dated. Other parts were worn out. We started to get irritated by its flaws. So we had to make a decision: What were we going to do about it?

Rather than moving again, we chose to invest in the house and improve it. Over the last few years, we've renovated the master bathroom and closet, the kitchen, parts of the living room, and the basement. And guess what? We fell back in love with our house. We discovered the Second Happy in the same house.

Don't Start Over—Get Better

The same thing can happen with a marriage. You can become less happy with it than you were when you started. But here's the great news: You don't need to end your marriage and look for another one to be happy again. You just need to invest in the relationship you have to find the *Second* Happy. That's really the way God designed marriage to be anyway. Lasting and fulfilling.

That's why Marcia and I wrote *The Second Happy*. We've been married for thirty-seven years—wow, even as we write those words, it seems hard to believe. First, because we don't feel that old. But second, and more important, because if you'd seen our marriage in the first few years, you probably would not have believed we would make it. You'll read about some of our struggles in this book. But by God's grace, our marriage is the best it's ever been in the nearly four decades we've been together. We've been through a lot, we've gleaned a lot, and we're living the Second Happy.

We want to share what we've learned with you. We distilled our most important lessons into seven practices that will make your marriage even better than your honeymoon—or if you're reading this and not yet married, it will set you up for a marriage that starts solid and remains happy.

These practices have memorable names, reveal a spiritual truth rooted in Scripture, and will help you repair, grow, strengthen, or prepare for your marriage. At the end of each practice, we've included questions for each of you to answer individually first and then to discuss as a couple. You'll also find group discussion questions you can use if you're going through this book with other couples. Whichever way you choose to use it, this book will point the way to your Second Happy.

Every Marriage Can Become Happier

No matter the age or stage of your relationship, we believe this book can help you.

IF YOU ARE OFFICIALLY DATING

As soon as your dating relationship becomes official and you are boyfriend and girlfriend, we recommend you put a conversation about faith on the table—before you try to build a one-of-a-kind relationship or think about marriage. We write about shared values in this book, but we recommend you first read my book *Grown-Up Faith: The Big Picture for a Bigger Life.*[1] It contains the answers to life's ten big questions. What you believe becomes the foundation of your faith—and your relationships. Once you're on the same page in your faith, read this book together to get a look ahead and learn what a strong, happy marriage looks like.

IF YOU ARE ENGAGED TO BE MARRIED

If you've made your engagement official, then this book would be a great part of your premarital counseling process. As you read and discuss the practices, focus especially on practice 1, "Break the Quit Cycle"; practice 3, "Pick a Fair Fight"; and practice 5, "Don't Settle for the Hollow Easter Bunny." These three practices frame how to develop an enduring marriage, how to process disagreement, and how to choose the values upon which you will build your marriage.

IF YOUR MARRIAGE IS ALREADY HAPPY

You already have a head start if your marriage is happy more of the time than it is unhappy. You're probably well prepared to answer the questions and engage in the discussion prompted by the "Conversation for a Couple" section at the end of each practice. We believe you will also be able to implement the seven practices quickly. You and your spouse might benefit from going through the book in a couples' small group to develop a greater sense of community. As you share your stories and growth with other couples who have challenges, they will be encouraged to stay engaged in the process.

IF YOUR MARRIAGE IS LESS HAPPY
THAN IT USED TO BE

If you are feeling especially challenged in your marriage or unhappy in your relationship, we *strongly* recommend that you and your spouse read this book as part of a small group of couples and not just on your own. It can be difficult to process honest questions when you're more unhappy than happy in your marriage. There is a huge benefit that comes with being in a community for mutual encouragement and the courage to go after developing a better relationship and a strong marriage. It may be hard, but it will be worth it!

IF YOU ARE EMPTY NESTERS

For some couples, the empty-nester season is one of the hardest times for their marriages, rivaling the early years of parenting. If that's where you are, don't take it lightly. Marcia and I have one child at home as well as three grown children who have left the nest, so this season is only a year away for us. Consider getting together with two to five other couples who are in the same season and read this book together. We believe the seven practices will help you perform a much-needed "renovation" during this season when some things in your marriage feel worn or out of style. Your coming retirement years can also be the happiest years of your marriage.

No matter where your marriage is—in trouble, lacking a spark, or solid but seeking to go to the next level—it can be helped by the practices in this book. Your marriage can get better no matter how good or bad it's been in the past. You can have a marriage where you really get along. Where you stop pretending. Where you truly love each other, treat each other with kindness every day, find ways to compromise that make you both happy, and never consider giving up.

Your marriage *can* be happy again. And here's the best news: the Second Happy of a sustained and deepened marriage is much better and richer than the first happy of the honeymoon. You just need to learn how to get there. The first practice will help you get started. So turn the page and begin the journey.

| | CONVERSATION FOR A COUPLE | |

Answer these questions on your own, with your spouse doing the same. Then make an appointment with each other to discuss your answers. Have an honest conversation with the goal of serving each other in order to develop a better marriage. Be honest with your feelings, but focus on how *you* can change by applying the practice described to yourself, not your spouse.

1. What was your level of happiness (contentment, joy, satisfaction) in your relationship with your spouse at each of these stages, with 1 representing hopeless and 10 totally happy?

Dating	1	2	3	4	5	6	7	8	9	10
Honeymoon	1	2	3	4	5	6	7	8	9	10
First Year of Marriage	1	2	3	4	5	6	7	8	9	10
At Its Lowest Point	1	2	3	4	5	6	7	8	9	10
Today	1	2	3	4	5	6	7	8	9	10

Be prepared to discuss why you chose those ratings with your spouse.

2. What would you identify as the most difficult problem or chal-lenge your relationship needs to overcome for the two of you to have a happy, healthy, fulfilling marriage?

3. What is your greatest hope for your marriage? Describe what your best relationship would look like.

4. Where do you most need to improve to make your relation-ship better?

Once you've shared your answers, discuss what each of you needs to do as a result of your conversation.

DISCUSSION FOR A SMALL GROUP

1. Introduce yourself by telling everyone your name, how long you've been married, your occupation, and one interesting or little-known fact about yourself.

2. How did you and your spouse meet? What attracted you to each other?

3. What prompted you to read *The Second Happy* and become a part of this group?

4. Which of the promises in the introduction is most appealing to you?
   - Really getting along
   - Stopping the pretending
   - Treating each other with kindness every day
   - Truly loving each other
   - Finding ways to compromise happily
   - Never considering giving up

5. What is your reaction to the idea of being able to invest in your marriage and "renovate" it to the point where you will be happier than you were on your honeymoon?

6. On a scale of 1 to 10, what is your level of hope for improving your marriage?

7. Did you answer the questions from "Conversation for a Couple" above individually and then talk to each other about your responses? If so, how did that go? What did you learn? If not, are you willing to commit to doing that for the introduction and practice 1 before the next meeting?

8. Finish this sentence: When we've finished this book, a *win* in our marriage would be _____.

Break the Quit Cycle

Each of the seven practices in this book will help you build—or rebuild—your marriage. But if you were to learn only one, this one would be the most important for sustaining your marriage. That's the reason we put it first. It's based on a simple picture, one that I can draw on a napkin. In fact, I often have. And the message in it is so powerful that it has been a tool to train Marcia and me, not only in our marriage but also in our careers, health, parenting, finances, and faith. This practice will not only change your marriage, it will change your life.

I learned about the core concept in a book titled *You Don't Have to Quit*, by Anne and Ray Ortlund.[1] The book is about how to have perseverance when you want to give up. That makes it a perfect tool for marriage.

Do You Know These ABCs?

Here's the picture. In life, every endeavor, project, job, team, organization, family, and relationship travels through three phases or zones: the A Zone, the B Zone, and the C Zone. It can be drawn this way:

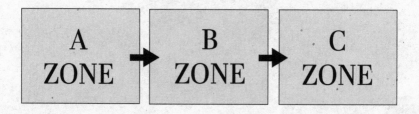

They represent the beginning, the middle, and the end of anything you attempt to do in life. As you live your life, you have to travel through these zones repeatedly.

THE A ZONE

The A Zone is where everything we look forward to begins. It's full of promise. It's the honeymoon phase. Everything is new and exciting. It's when we buy the new car and everything is perfect. It's when we get the job or have the grand opening or buy the new house. It's the first day of college. It's the opening day of football, baseball, or soccer season—pick your sport. It's the new toy, furniture, motorcycle, clothes. You get the idea. It's the actual honeymoon after the wedding ceremony. It's the starting line, full of hope, energy, and expectation.

> In life, every endeavor . . . travels through three phases or zones: the A Zone, the B Zone, and the C Zone.

Most important: it's free of baggage. Like a new season in sports, it starts with no losses. Everyone loves the A Zone. We want to live in the A Zone. It's the dream stage of every project, relationship, career, and season. As you read this, we bet you're thinking of the next wonderful thing you're looking forward to, and it confirms in your heart and mind that you love A Zones. We all do.

| A ZONE FULL OF PROMISE | B ZONE | C ZONE |

Marcia and I look back on our relational A Zone and smile. Our dating life was a fantastic A Zone. Yours probably was too. Marcia and I met in college. Back then, roller-skating was still popular. Marcia says the roller rink is where she first saw me. But of course, we each have our own side of the story:

MARCIA: As I was standing in line at the roller rink, just ahead of me was an upperclassman with an Afro. This was the '80s. I thought to myself, *He's cute. But he's so loud and obnoxious. I could never be interested in him.*

KEVIN: I don't remember seeing Marcia at the skating rink. However, when I did finally meet her, I did everything in my power to win her over.

MARCIA: As God would have it, I encountered Kevin the very next Sunday. Of all the churches in our college town, I happened to visit the one where he was serving as an intern. He actually led the college Bible study. And I have to say that I was impressed. My heart softened a bit.

KEVIN: It was obvious right away that we were an "opposites attract" couple. I was more the extrovert and she was more the introvert.

MARCIA: I was more studious, and he was more—well, less studious.

KEVIN: Except in my major.

MARCIA: But we had a lot in common, including our faith upbringing, our love for adventure, and our interest in movies.

KEVIN: I was headed into a career as a pastor. Marcia planned to be a schoolteacher. Eighteen months after we met, she accepted my proposal for marriage. We just knew we were going to have an awesome A-Zone life together.

MARCIA: Our wedding took place in my small hometown of Croswell, Michigan, in the church where I was raised. We were surrounded by my family, friends, and church members who had known me my whole life. It was a beautiful ceremony on a picture-perfect day.

On August 7, 1982, we tied the knot, and our adventure began the next day as we left for our long-awaited honeymoon. Our plan was to drive our ten-year-old Volkswagen Beetle to the Pocono Mountains of Pennsylvania. I was—and still am—a car guy, but we had to settle for an old bug with its thirty-four-brake-horsepower engine and top speed of seventy-one miles per hour. It was all we could afford.

We left Michigan for Pennsylvania the morning after the wedding. This was back before Siri, GPS, or any other mobile technology. You couldn't just punch in an address and get turn-by-turn directions. Maps were available, but I told Marcia we didn't need one. We would simply follow the big green road signs to our destination. How hard could it be?

I found out soon after we crossed into the next state. I remember seeing a sign that said it was seventy miles to the next major city. But after we traveled for an hour, we passed the same sign. Not one like it. The same one. Somehow I had taken us in a circle. So I did what all *real* men do: I kept driving without getting directions.

Eventually we made it to Pennsylvania. But then we faced a new challenge. It had never occurred to me that our old Beetle would have a hard time in the mountains. With the pedal to the floor and the engine wide open, we averaged thirty-five miles per hour going uphill. It was horrible—and hilarious.

After a while we managed to get into the vicinity of the "resort" (I use that term loosely), but we simply could not find it. Finally, I swallowed my pride, stopped, and asked for directions. Multiple times. But our destination was so obscure that nobody knew where it was. We kept driving around, and we started to believe we'd mailed our money to a phony address.

We did eventually find our honeymoon hideaway, which was quite literally hidden away. As bad as the trip was getting there, it was well worth it. We had a great honeymoon. It was a wonderful first week together as we felt the thrill of spending every minute with each other. But of course, traveling home, we faced more challenges. The Beetle's muffler fell off. When we'd stop at a tollbooth and roll down the window, the roar of the engine was deafening, and the tollbooth worker would cringe. We can laugh about it now, but at the time it was really embarrassing.

Our adventures continued into the early days of our marriage. The poor VW didn't even last a year after the wedding. One day as we drove away from our apartment, we heard the car backfire. When I glanced at the rearview mirror, I saw fire coming up from the engine. We jumped out of the car right as it burst into flames. Too bad we didn't have our iPhones in those days. We could have taken a great video to show our "someday" kids.

In our second year of marriage, we bought our first house. It was old, but it was ours. We entertained ourselves with cheap fun like visits to Cedar Point amusement park or activities in the great outdoors. With both of us working and without kids, we fit the term *dinks* (dual income no kids). While we did enjoy some really good friends and a great church, the honeymoon phase was fading fast. We didn't know it then, but we were approaching the B Zone.

THE B ZONE

Everything in life that starts with an A Zone, including marriage, gives way to a B Zone. While the A Zone is full of promise, the B Zone is full of problems. It's the phase when life gets hard, sometimes so hard you wonder if the goal you started out to achieve is really worth the effort.

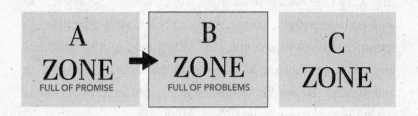

When Marcia and I bought our house, which was an A-Zone moment, I was excited about doing some things to fix it up. Are you familiar with Home Depot's "You can do it, we can help" slogan? Well, I believe that's nothing more than an A-Zone media ploy designed to suck us into home projects that we *believe* are easily doable. But the reality is that you end up making forty-seven trips to Home Depot, and with each trip, you descend deeper into the problems of the B Zone. The more money and time you spend, the more aggravated you feel. I can't tell you the number of times I've gotten partway through a dream project that has become a nightmare I just don't care about anymore.

If you stay in *anything* long enough, you will find yourself in the B Zone. The problems always come. Your brand-new car quickly becomes a used car, but you're still paying new-car payments. The new job becomes a grind, as do the college classes. The sports season doesn't turn out the way you hoped. The new toy breaks. The furniture gets worn out. So do the clothes.

> While the A Zone is full of promise, the B Zone is full of problems. It's the phase when life gets hard.

What's true of home projects and other activities is true in marriage. Every marriage passes through a honeymoon season. What do we say weeks or months after the wedding? *The honeymoon is over.* What was once easy sailing has become an uphill climb. It's hard. The knight in shining armor falls off his horse. The once-fair lady becomes the ball and chain. Welcome to the B Zone.

What happens when our B-Zone disappointments eclipse our A-Zone dreams? We want to go to the Q Zone. *Wait*, you may be thinking, *you didn't mention a Q Zone! What's the Q Zone?* That's where we quit.

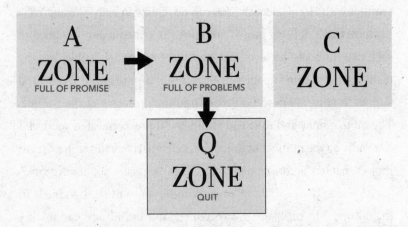

All around my house are half-finished projects I started with great intentions but that ended up in the Q Zone. They're proof that when A-Zone wishes hit B-Zone walls, the easiest thing to do is go to the Q Zone. But that's the road to failure. If you Q Zone enough things, it becomes a habit. We chase the excitement of A Zones, feel the stress of B Zones, escape to the Q Zones, and then go looking for new A Zones because that's what excites us and makes us feel good.

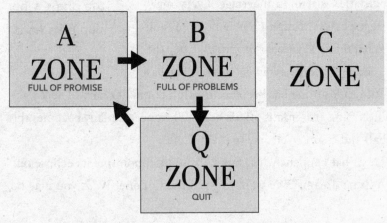

The problem is that *every* A Zone leads to a B Zone, and if you always go to the Q Zone when that happens, you develop an addictive cycle of quitting. The pattern creates short-term relationships, shortcut habits, and short attention spans. That's why so many people live in chaos and failure. They are experiencing the wreckage of multiple Q-Zone decisions: unfinished educational degrees, incomplete jobs, derailed careers, chaotic finances, underdeveloped faith, half-built marriages.

> If you Q Zone enough things, it becomes a habit.

Why does this matter? What do we lose when we go to the Q Zone? Well, we lose the most worthwhile things in life: long-term relationships, long-term health, financial stability, deep and rewarding faith. As my mentor and friend John Maxwell says, "Everything worthwhile is uphill."[2] You have to work your way through the B Zones of life to get life's greatest rewards. Giving in to the Q Zone is like an NFL prospect experiencing the A-Zone excitement of being drafted and getting a contract, and then quitting during training camp. That player can never win a Super Bowl, experience the camaraderie of the team, or even gain the experience of playing in a real NFL game!

Marcia and I experienced the B Zone big-time from year two to year four of our marriage. We really understood what the phrase "the honeymoon is over" meant, because we were often locked in spiteful conflict. Sometimes we would call a truce, and we would have the best of times—for a few days. But those days were often followed by the worst of times. Here's how we remember it:

KEVIN: By the third or fourth year I was saying to Marcia, "You're nicer to people at work, at church, and in public than you are to me at home. At home you're just stubborn and mean."

MARCIA: And I was saying, "Well, *Pastor*, you listen and care for other people, but when you get home, you're controlling and trying to change who I am."

We didn't understand what was going on at the time. Nobody had shown us the picture of the ABC Zones of life. All we knew was that we were at each other's throats—or you could call it mutual irritation due to unmet expectations. We were descending into deep disappointment with each other.

It all came to a head one day during a blowup at a grocery store. Of course, neither of us can remember what we fought over, but we do remember the emotion. If we walked into that store even today, after more than thirty years, we could take you to the exact spot where we embarrassed ourselves: in the frozen food section just past the milk coolers.

Our screaming match was as chilly as the freezers. It was the accumulation of all the spats we'd had up until then, and it broke the dam. Our memories are vivid:

KEVIN: I stormed out of the store and walked the couple of blocks home. I was fuming. I was tired of being married to this woman who was a whole lot easier to date than to marry. I was losing myself and feeling imprisoned.

MARCIA: I was left to do the shopping, feeling all alone and defeated. I drove the short distance home and decided to ignore Kevin for as long as I could.

KEVIN: That was the first time I said to myself, "Well, now I know why my parents divorced. Because the reality of marriage sucks." And even though I swore I'd never get divorced, I wondered, *Can we make it? What if I married the wrong person?*

MARCIA: In the heat of the grocery store moment, I remember thinking that maybe divorce was the only option we had left. I certainly didn't want a divorce. While Kevin's personality is prone to more highs and lows, mine is steady. My highs are not as high, and my lows are not as low. So I wanted to get things worked out. I tried to tell myself, "It really isn't that bad, is it?" But the truth was that I was utterly defeated. I didn't know where else to turn.

KEVIN: Soon enough, God interrupted my thinking and said, *Kevin, do not comfort yourself with the thought of quitting. Divorce is not an option for you. You need to learn how to love someone other than yourself.*

God's voice wasn't audible; it was more of a distinct impression upon my spirit. But God could not have been clearer even if he *had* spoken audibly. Sadly, I didn't completely stop comforting myself with the idea of quitting until I had a moment with my mom. Yes, I went home, crying to Mom. I knew *she* would understand. After all, she had been in a disappointing marriage for sixteen years until she and my dad finally divorced. She had become a single mom with four kids—living with two of them after my older brothers went to live with Dad. She was trying to survive as a thirty-three-year-old high school dropout with no work experience, living in government-subsidized housing with my younger sister and me. That experience had made Mom and me tight, so I was confident she would support me, her son, who was stuck with a selfish wife.

I'll never forget that moment. As I was crying to her about Marcia, Mom said, "Son, I understand. You brought a lot of baggage into your marriage. You need to grow up. You've got a good one in Marcia, so go back home and learn to be a better husband."

What? Even my mom had been duped by Marcia!

I drove home thinking, *Nobody knows what I have to live with at home.* Yes, I really thought that at the time. I believed in my heart that the primary problem was Marcia. If God would just fix Marcia, we'd be fine. Sure, I've got some issues. But hers are *huge* compared to mine. So I often prayed, "God, help Marcia get over her self-centeredness." But God was not answering my prayers, because I was the problem. I just couldn't see it.

When you're in the B Zone, you can lose track of why you even started the journey. Your vision gets cloudy.

MARCIA: Recently I took a trip to Seattle with Jake, our third child, who's in his midtwenties. We decided to hike to the top of Mount Si, a mountain with great views of Mount Rainier, which was about forty-five minutes outside the city. The climb was four miles. When we started, it was raining, but the weather report indicated the rain would be stopping soon. However, as we climbed mile after mile, the rain kept on coming. Even when we reached the top, it was still raining, and foggy mist was so thick we could only see about ten feet in front of us. There were no beautiful views, only wet clothes and pure exhaustion. Plus a soggy four-mile hike back down the mountain. Talk about a B-Zone experience. The payoff at the end, the C Zone we'd hoped for, never happened. No one wants to go through life like that.

Honestly, one of the most devastating impacts of any B Zone is the dense fog it puts over the future. The B Zone makes it nearly impossible to see the summit at the top of the mountain. You lose the vision. And yet it is the top of the mountain that inspires us to make the climb. Jake and I summited Mount Si to see the view. In our marriages the C Zone is the promise of a lifetime of companionship, a fifty-year wedding anniversary, being lovers for life, and perhaps even the hope of great kids and a legacy of grandkids.

But the B Zone brings storms to the mountain. Dark clouds descend and you can't see the vision anymore. The dream becomes blurred, and you wonder why you are even in this relationship. *Is it really worth it?* you ask yourself. The Q Zone looks very appealing in those moments.

And let's be honest. There are more ways to quit than just filing for divorce. Many of us Q Zone on the very things that made our relationship work in the beginning. In our marriage, Marcia and I stopped doing the things we had done as expressions of love while dating. They faded more and more as we descended into the B Zone.

People usually quit on the small stuff before they quit on the big stuff. Little Q Zones accumulate and increase the discouragement of the B Zone. If we lose hope, the B Zone wins.

THE C ZONE

If you draw a line, refuse to enter the Q Zone, and continue to climb uphill, you can persevere through the B Zone and finally reach the C Zone. Where the B Zone is the middle of training camp two-a-day practices, the wall in the marathon, the second year of a four-year degree, and the worst grind of a job that feels like it will never end, the C Zone is the reward for a job well done. It's the championship trophy, the finish-line party, the degree earned, the promotion to your dream job, the wedding anniversary after five, twenty-five, or even fifty years. It's heaven with God for eternity after your life on earth is done. If you hang in there through the B Zone, you go from promise to problems to payoffs.

> People usually quit on the small stuff before they quit on the big stuff.

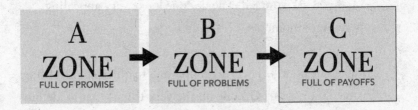

A ZONE
FULL OF PROMISE

→ B ZONE
FULL OF PROBLEMS

→ C ZONE
FULL OF PAYOFFS

It takes self-awareness and a lot of courage to examine our actions and confess that we're quitting on the small things. But if we stay engaged, keep the vision for the C Zone alive, continue working, and refuse to Q Zone even in small ways, we can experience the payoff of the C Zone. If the A Zone is an awesome vision, and the B Zone is being bone-weary, then the C Zone is celebration time.

The ABCs of a Great Marriage

So now that you understand the picture, how can this help your marriage? How did learning about the three zones help Marcia and me turn our marriage from disappointing to lasting? It taught us to do the following three things.

1. BUILD B-ZONE MUSCLE

If a husband and wife learn the lesson of how to build B-Zone muscle, they can be great friends and lovers for life. How do you build that muscle? The answer can be found in John 13. The night before his crucifixion, Jesus and his disciples had gathered in a room to celebrate the Passover meal. Jesus knew this was the end of his time on earth. He was about to fulfill his purpose of giving his life to save ours, his death paying our sin debt and allowing us to be restored to God.

When everyone arrived at the dinner that night, the normal custom of having their feet washed had not occurred. Expecting to have their feet washed may sound odd to us because there is no exact modern equivalent. Today, we greet people who come to our home, take their coats, and offer them a drink. In Jesus's days, people wore open sandals and walked on streets of dirt and dust. So when people came inside to gather for dinner, their feet were filthy. I mean offensive. And they didn't sit in chairs with their feet tucked safely under the table the way we do. They reclined at a low table, so their feet would have been really close to one another. Are you getting why guests' feet needed to be washed? That unpleasant job was usually given to a very low-level servant. But when the disciples gathered, there was no servant there to wash anyone's feet.

What happened next was the lesson of a lifetime for the disciples. Jesus took a basin of water and a towel and began performing the task. You can imagine how the disciples must have frozen in silent disbelief. Here was the Messiah, the Lord of lords, the One who created the universe, doing the job of the lowest servant. Instead of being served, he was serving! Scripture says,

> When he [Jesus] had finished washing their feet, he put on his clothes and returned to his place. "Do you understand what I have done for you?" he asked them. "You call me 'Teacher' and 'Lord,' and rightly so, for that is what I am. Now that I, your Lord and Teacher, have washed your feet, *you also should wash one another's feet.* I have set you an example that you should do as I have done for you. Very truly I tell you, no servant is greater than his master, nor is a messenger greater than the one who sent him. Now that you know these things, *you will be blessed if you do them.*" (John 13:12–17, emphasis added)

What's the one lesson? The one that will change your life and marriage? "Wash one another's feet."

No, not literally. You don't need to pull out a basin and a towel to wash each other's feet before dinner. But you do need to live with a disposition of service toward each other. This message from Jesus wasn't just for the twelve guys whose feet he washed. Nor was it just a church thing for leaders. It was a model for everyone who ever desires to follow Jesus and be like him.

If you want to have a good marriage, you need to get over being self-serving and build your relationship through self-sacrifice. You need to get over your own self-interest and look after the interests of your spouse. Expect to be the servant, not the served, in your marriage. Build this one muscle, and your marriage will be blessed. It's the essence of love.

I could not love Marcia well in the early days because I was too concerned about how well Marcia loved me. And Marcia could not love me well because she was too concerned about how I was loving her. Self-interest has an almost unlimited number of ways to justify its existence. It keeps score and always concludes that the other person hasn't done enough.

The B-Zone muscle I needed to build in my marriage was the strength to die to my self-interest and serve Marcia's interests first. And she needed to do the same. We both had to learn to love like Jesus, who said, "Greater love has no one than this: to lay down one's life for one's friends" (John 15:13). If I was going to love Marcia, that was the standard I had to meet. As the apostle Paul, inspired by the Holy Spirit, wrote, "I'm bankrupt without love. Love never gives up. Love cares more for others than for self. . . . [Love] isn't always 'me first'" (1 Cor. 13:3–5 THE MESSAGE).

In the early years of our marriage, if I had substituted my name for *love* in that passage, I'd have fallen way short: "Kevin never gives up. Kevin cares more for Marcia than for self. . . . Kevin isn't always 'me-first.'" I had not developed the muscle for real love. To have a good marriage, to regain the happiness I felt in the A Zone, I needed the Holy Spirit to train me to wash my wife's feet as a normal way of relating to her. I needed to learn to put her interests first, not my own. And she would have to do the same.

If you don't learn and live this one lesson, then your marriage will be bankrupt. Metaphorically washing your spouse's feet creates B-Zone muscle so that you can have a C-Zone marriage.

2. DEVELOP C-ZONE HOPE

It can be hard to have C-Zone hope when you're stuck in the middle of a B-Zone season of marriage. That's especially true for couples who have been living in a B-Zone marriage for so long they believe they are done.

Have you ever had someone encourage you to "keep at it" when you were exhausted? I mean bone-weary done? I once had a fitness trainer whose primary benefit to me was pushing me past the B Zone and keeping me out of the Q Zone. I discovered he could help me do 10 to 20 percent more reps per set than I would do on my own. He pushed me past exhaustion. And at the end of each set, I felt free to tell him how much I hated him.

What Marcia and I want to do is coach you so you will keep doing more reps. You're capable of more than you think is possible. You can build B-Zone muscle. And here's what's most important: you don't have to do it on your own. God will supernaturally help you. If you will lean into him, he will do for you what you cannot do for yourself. If you trust him, he will help you develop C-Zone hope.

That may be hard to believe when you are weary, when you're at the end of yourself, when you're tired of doing reps. You may hate the person who says, "Don't quit." Okay, fair enough. Feel free to hate us right now. Like my trainer at the gym, we don't mind. We're here to coach you. Hate us—and then do some more reps.

A couple we know, Bill and Susan, were at the point where they thought their marriage was over. They couldn't imagine doing one more rep. They had tried everything they knew to do, but nothing worked. The damage was done. The marriage was a dead horse. The ride was over. They thought it would be unhealthy for their kids to be around parents who had married the wrong person and had grown apart. They believed it would be better to just confess that their marriage was over, divorce each other, and build a good, loving relationship with the kids separately.

That was their plan. But they also knew divorce would have a huge negative impact on their kids. So to provide some sort of support system for them when the divorce hit, they decided to look for a church. It was the only place they could think of to provide a softer landing place for their kids.

Bill and Susan were not followers of Jesus, and they had no personal interest in faith. But they had heard of 12Stone Church, so they attended to connect their kids into a community before they split. While they waited for their kids to build relationships, they were invited to a small-group-based program to strengthen marriages called Re|Engage. They figured, why not? It can't hurt. After all, they were already working on their divorce papers.

One of the first principles they learned was to draw a circle around yourself, and work on changing everyone inside the circle.[3] They were told not to try to change the other person, but to each work on themselves. So they did. In the process, they also learned about the love of God and how Jesus died for their sin to offer forgiveness and restoration. God's love was mind-blowing to them. Bill and Susan accepted Christ and started to transform from the inside out. Having received grace from God, they became better at giving grace to each other.

Where did this lead? The dead horse of their marriage rose from the dead! They gained hope, not only for their marriage but for having a family that would experience love like they had never known. They tore up the divorce papers and worked on their marriage, learning to wash each other's feet. They stayed together and even added a third child to the family. Now they help other couples improve their marriages by leading groups like the one they were in.

That's the power of God. The hope of Christ can help us develop C-Zone hope. Getting to the C Zone in marriage is possible for any couple who receives God's love and follows Jesus. Does that magically make the B Zone easy? No. But with B-Zone muscle and C-Zone hope, we can keep moving forward instead of quitting.

3. PRACTICE B-ZONE REPS

Marcia is a good athlete, and in recent years she's become a dedicated runner—a real runner who runs marathons. In early 2020 she did the Dopey Challenge at Walt Disney World. Over four successive days she ran a 5K, a 10K, a half marathon, and a marathon. I can't even fathom that. I hate running. Every now and then, I'll join Marcia for a short jog, but that's because I love Marcia, not running. It's foot washing for me. I prefer to lift weights, which I've done on and off my whole life. To keep building muscle, I do reps. The equivalent for Marcia is putting in miles.

Developing B-Zone muscle is like getting in physical shape. You have to put in your miles or do your reps. It requires you to develop the right habits. Here are some examples of things we do for each other to practice our reps. They may give you ideas for how to serve your spouse.

MARCIA: As with anything worthwhile, developing B-Zone muscle is easier said than done. Here are a few practical things that have worked for me. Hopefully they'll give you a starting place to develop your own practices.

Put Yourself in Your Spouse's Shoes

You can serve anyone by treating them kindly and doing for them what you would want done for you. But if you really want to serve your spouse, you have to find the things that make them feel special, that say "I am serving you." That may be different from what you would want done for you. If you do what *you* like, then you're only making *yourself* happy.

Not long ago, Kevin received a half-zip sport pullover from a group for whom he had done a leadership talk. He really liked that pullover. It fit him well and was just right for in-between weather. One day he couldn't find it. You can imagine the searching that took place—in the laundry, through all rooms of the house, at the office, and in each of our vehicles. But it was nowhere to be found. For a couple of weeks we hoped it would turn up, but we finally gave up our search and he lamented it.

I decided to secretly get in contact with the person who had given it to him and ask for a couple of more. I surprised Kevin with them, and, boy, was he happy. It made his day. He felt I was the most thoughtful, beautiful, loving wife a man could have. And every time he puts on the pullover, I have the satisfaction of knowing that I served him well.

> "Invest the time and effort to put yourself in your spouse's shoes."

I encourage you to invest the time and effort to put yourself in your spouse's shoes. What would they appreciate? What would make them feel loved? A special meal? A foot rub? A night with their friends? Very often the simple things are the things that make us feel most loved.

Believe the Best of Your Spouse

Another thing I do is always give Kevin the benefit of the doubt. When something happens that I don't like or he says something that rubs me the wrong way, I tell myself he didn't intend for me to take it the way I did. That immediately defuses the situation before it can escalate. Then if I think I need clarification or an explanation, I'll bring it up later when the intensity of my feelings has passed. Almost always it turns out to be a matter of perspective. Once he gives me his reasoning and I give him mine, the problem gets resolved, and we have another marital success. That builds muscle and develops hope.

Take Your Emotions to God First

Prayer is really the glue that holds marriages together. If I'm feeling neglected, taken advantage of, in need of a break, or annoyed, or if I'm taking offense at everything Kevin does, feeling overwhelmed at the *unfairness* of it all or like he can't do anything right—the list could go on and on—I take it before my Father in prayer. I pour out my heart to him. All of my thoughts, even if I know they don't make sense or are overly negative. I ask him to give me perspective. God invariably reminds me that Kevin is not perfect, and neither am I. Often when I feel frustrated, it's because I'm putting Kevin in the place where God needs to be. Only God is perfect.

Our spouses were never meant to be put on a pedestal or fill God's place in our lives. The more time we spend with God, praying and reading his Word, the more our hearts can be open to our spouses. Ninety-nine percent of the time when I'm not happy with Kevin, all I have to do is take it to God. If I *do* have a legitimate concern, I first pray that God will work in Kevin, and then we eventually talk it through and work it out. We are honest, kind, and candid.

KEVIN: Here are a few important practices that took me a while to learn. By sharing with you what I've done wrong and how I've worked to improve, I hope to help you build B-Zone muscle and gain successes that develop your C-Zone hope.

Respect Your Spouse's Point of View

As an extrovert, I have always loved having people over to the house. But it proved to be one of our re-occurring flare-ups. For example, we might be in conversation with some new friends and I'd say, "Hey, you guys doing anything right now? Why don't you come over and hang out?" If they accepted my invitation, Marcia would get annoyed, resulting in an undercurrent of tension all evening. After the friends left, I'd say, "You ruined the evening!" I couldn't understand why she wouldn't just relax and be hospitable.

As I was learning to wash her feet, I started to take the focus off of myself and think about her first. Instead of criticizing her for being unsociable or inhospitable, I tried to understand her. When I did that, I began to understand the issue wasn't hospitality; it was planning.

Whenever I invited people on the spur of the moment, Marcia was embarrassed because she didn't have sufficient time to get the house ready or to prepare food. I was making her look bad. As I write this now, it seems so obvious, but it wasn't obvious to me then. As soon as I understood her point of view, I changed my behavior.

We came to an understanding that I would invite people only when we had agreed to it ahead of time so that everything would be ready. Or we would plan ahead to have everything ready on a particular night, so that I was then free to invite anyone I wanted on the spur of the moment. Washing her feet meant starting from what mattered to her, and then going forward. It was a breakthrough change for both of us.

Give Your Spouse the Extras

In the early days of marriage, we lived on a spartan budget. I mean it was tight and the margins were small. So I was excited whenever I'd do a wedding or speak at an event and receive an honorarium. It was never much, but fifty dollars in those days felt like freedom. Since that money was not in the budget as expected income, I didn't have to account for it. It was my personal stash to use for fun.

Then one day I heard a pastor teach about loving his wife, and one of the illustrations he gave was that he gave her all the side money that came his way from speaking. As you can imagine, I thought that was a horrible idea. So I quickly and vehemently dismissed it.

God did not. He kept putting the thought in my mind. *If I really love Marcia like I say I do, wouldn't I put her first?* Reluctantly I reconsidered the idea and eventually practiced it. To my surprise, as I gained maturity, it became a joy to me. It was more fulfilling to give her a bit of financial freedom than it was to have it myself.

> "When you get an idea or a prompt to serve your spouse . . . and you obey it, it changes you *and* your marriage."

Let me pause and say something really important that I don't want you to miss. Don't ignore these kinds of prompts from God. They can be game changers. When you get an idea or a prompt to serve your spouse—especially one you want to deny or dismiss—and you obey it, it changes you *and* your marriage. Kindness begets kindness and fosters the joy of companionship. When we're both practicing B-Zone serving, we experience more and more C Zones together.

Find Little Ways to Serve

That brings me to the third practice. You may or may not agree with this, but it has helped me. Putting Marcia first means opening all doors for her, including the car door. It means making sure she has hot water in the shower. It means getting her something to drink before getting one for myself. It means cleaning the snow off her car in winter. (Okay, that was when we lived in Michigan.) You get the idea. I discovered that if I consistently served her in little things, I was less likely to quit on the big things. Growing B-Zone muscle meant being diligent in the practice of putting Marcia first in the little things.

Following these practices did not stop us from having B-Zone issues or seasons. But we discovered that instead of drifting toward the Q Zone, we developed B-Zone muscle, which enabled us to keep climbing. We were building a new level of endurance that helped us persevere through more challenging issues. It gave us the strength to maintain and even grow in our marriage while we planted a church, faced near bankruptcy, added four kids, and weathered other storms. And we developed even greater C-Zone hope, because we had experienced some C-Zone wins on proverbial mountaintops where the payoffs were picture perfect. True, some climbs felt more like Mount Si, where it was foggy and soggy, and we knew we'd have to scale the mountain again another day to see the view. But that was okay, because we knew that every day we were climbing together and working for each other's best. We knew from experience that there would be greater celebration days ahead.

Grab Your Towel and Basin

A good marriage is like a good family, a good neighborhood, a good business, or a good team. The people are unselfish. They serve one another. They follow the example of Jesus and wash one another's feet.

In this practice we have written boldly about how God has led us to serve each other and how his power gives us strength to climb the mountain of marriage. You do not have to be a follower of Jesus to benefit from the ABC Zones—or to learn from the six practices to come. But we invite you to reflect seriously on faith. God loves you, and he wants you to have a relationship with him. If you have questions about God and are looking for answers, we recommend the previously mentioned book, *Grown-Up Faith*. It explains the foundations upon which we have built our lives.

Whether you are a follower of Jesus, a practicer of another faith, an agnostic, or an atheist, you cannot escape the B Zones of life or in your marriage. Therefore, you have to make the decision. Will you do what's needed in order to reach and enjoy the C Zone? If not, you will likely default your way into the Q Zone and then go searching for another A Zone. Don't get stuck in a cycle that never takes you where you really want to go. If you are in the B Zone in marriage, the only way to work your way out is by serving your spouse and putting them first. What will you choose to do?

CONVERSATION FOR A COUPLE

Answer these questions on your own, with your spouse doing the same. Then make an appointment with each other to discuss your answers. Have an honest conversation with the goal of serving each other in order to develop a better marriage. Be honest with your feelings, but focus on how *you* can change by applying the practice to yourself, not your spouse.

1. What is the B Zone in your marriage? The issue or area that frustrates you the most, because you don't seem to be able to make progress? How does it make you feel? Why is it important that you work through it?

2. How long has this been a problem? Can you remember when and how it started? What is the most recent example you can think of?

3. What is your C-Zone hope for this problem? What would a win look like for you and how would you celebrate it?

4. What could you do to change that would help in this area? What actions could you take beginning today to wash your spouse's feet and remove your contribution to this problem?

Once you've shared your answers, discuss what each of you needs to do as a result of your conversation.

DISCUSSION FOR A SMALL GROUP

1. What's the best celebration you've ever been a part of? Why was it significant or special to you?

2. In life, do B Zones usually take you by surprise or do you expect them and plan for them? Explain.

3. When you enter a new A Zone, how do you decide whether the C-Zone goal will be worth fighting through the B Zone to reach it?

4. How are B Zones in marriage different from B Zones in other areas of life, such as careers, hobbies, finances, and so on?

5. What is the hardest thing about washing other people's feet and putting them first? How do you get yourself to do it when you don't want to?

6. Is washing your spouse's feet easier or more difficult than washing someone else's? Why?

7. If you answered the questions from "Conversation for a Couple" above, how did it go?

8. What change in your actions did you identify that you need to make to put your spouse first? What will you do differently to make that change? When will you do it?

PRACTICE 2

Get Your Hands Up

A man in his early forties walked up to me after I had spoken to a room full of leaders at 12Stone Church, where I'm the founding pastor. He said his name was Brian, and he wanted to tell me his story. But the way he started really caught me off guard.

"My life was ruined by a question," he said, and then he paused.

"Okay, what was the question?" I asked.

"Are you happy? The question 'Are you happy?' ruined my life."

That caught my attention, so I asked him to explain.

Brian said he thought our culture was constantly telling us we should ask ourselves this question, that it was the benchmark for life.

> Maybe I'm very aware of this because I've struggled with trying to be happy my entire life. I found myself questioning my happiness in every area of my life, including my marriage. Ultimately, this took me down a very negative road. I went from asking myself, "Am I happy in my marriage?" to asking myself, "Is

Rachel making me happy?" to telling myself, "She *should* make me happy!" which turned into, "She's making me *un*happy." And anytime she did anything that didn't please me, I started telling myself, "I'm in an unhappy marriage."

What do people do when they're not happy with something? They throw everything away and start over. So that's what I did. I divorced my wife. I believed I would be leaving unhappiness behind. But not long after the divorce, guess what I realized? I still wasn't happy! I was alone, far from my young child, and less happy than I had been in my "unhappy" marriage! I thought, *What have I done?* It was a gut-wrenching moment when I realized that living your life by asking yourself "Am I happy?" all the time creates an insane, self-destructive cycle. It makes our feelings the center of our world and reinforces our natural self-centeredness.

I Surrender—But I Don't Give Up

Brian said a friend saw how miserable and broken he was and gave him some advice. He told Brian he needed to pray. Raised Catholic, Brian had never been religious.

"Praying seemed like a small, insignificant action for such a large, significant mess. But that's what I started to do. I asked God for help," said Brian. "At first my prayers were very selfish. But soon they changed. I knew I had made my own choices and my situation was my own fault. My prayers changed from 'Make me happy' to

'Jesus, I'm so sorry. Please help me. I don't know what to do. I'll listen and do what you tell me.'"

Brian felt miserable, but he believed he should keep praying. One day he spotted a chapel at a church not far from his office and started going there to pray during his lunch break or after work. "I was not particularly good at it, and I had no real plan or endgame in mind," he said. "But I was diligent in stopping by to pray. It didn't seem like it was helping, but I kept at it."

Then on his drive home from work, Brian believed God was prompting him to call his mother-in-law to apologize for what he had done to her daughter.

"That was not something I wanted to do, but I felt compelled," he said. "So I had a decision to make. Do I pull off the road and make the call or do I dismiss it? I pulled off the road and called her. That was humbling. It didn't really seem to resolve anything, but I at least felt I had honored God."

Meanwhile, God was doing something in his ex-wife, Rachel, too. She had been invited to 12Stone by a friend and was working on growing in her faith. When Brian found out, he asked her if he could go as well.

"Do what you want," she responded.

He did.

"For a while I sat two rows behind her," said Brian. "Then in the same row. And eventually next to her. In time I got up the courage to ask her out on a date, and she said yes. I know, it sounds strange, dating your ex-wife. We started going to a counselor and learning how to communicate. And I continued to pray. Along the way we became devoted followers of Jesus. The end of the story is that after twenty months of separation, we remarried! By God's grace, what my selfishness and blindness destroyed, God restored through his mercy and goodness."

Nobody is happy all the time. That's not realistic. Even the Second Happy marriage that Marcia and I have—and we believe you can have—isn't hearts and roses every minute of the day. It has its ups and downs. But it can be deeper and more content than the thrill of the honeymoon and last a lot longer.

Brian now recognizes that back before he divorced Rachel, he had been chasing something impossible, which got him stuck. But when he started praying, God woke him up and started to transform him. He might not always feel happy, but his life is now filled with a deeper joy and a stronger sense of purpose. He says that, thanks to Jesus, he is now an entirely different person. And because he knows God answers prayers, he prays with even greater passion and diligence than ever before.

The Seen and Unseen Battles

Brian and Rachel experienced a dramatic transformation thanks to prayer. When they couldn't get along, they each turned to God, put up their hands in surrender, and admitted they didn't have the power to save their marriage. They begged God to help them and he did. They won their marriage battle because they asked God to fight for them.

Most people underestimate the power of prayer, and they don't understand it. They see it as a religious activity, separate from the other parts of their lives. They think there is a wall dividing the spiritual world from the physical world. But those two worlds—the unseen and the seen—cannot be separated. Those two worlds always work together and influence each other. If you want to have a successful marriage, you need to knock down that imaginary wall and enlist God's help through prayer so you can win everyday battles.

The best picture in Scripture of this interaction between the spiritual and physical can be seen in Exodus 17. That's where we learned the practice we teach here for building a lasting happy marriage. Let me set the stage: Joshua, Moses's right-hand man, commanded the Israelites for the first time in battle. The fighting was fierce. He must have been horrified to see his brothers-in-arms dying beside him. As the leader, it would be his job to tell each dead man's wife that her husband wasn't coming home from the battle. Would Joshua be reminded of the battle every day he saw his friends' children growing up without their fathers?

He may have wondered, *How did I get here? Why do I have to fight when God is capable of performing miracles?* Joshua had seen plenty of miracles. He had seen the Israelites miraculously freed from slavery, with the Egyptians handing them gold on their way out. He had seen meek Moses, once a prince of Egypt, raise his staff and part the Red Sea. He had seen Pharaoh's army destroyed as the Red Sea closed over them. He had seen a pillar of fire traveling in the desert, water flowing from a rock, and manna falling from heaven. Yet, here he was, fighting a battle alongside a group of men who were physically strong but had not been trained to be an army.

Joshua was facing the Amalekites, a ruthless tribe of desert nomads known for killing whoever stood in their way and taking possession of their livestock and goods. When he went down to fight, he may have thought this was going to be a quick victory by God's hand. But it wasn't going that way. In fact, for a while it looked like the Israelites were going to lose. It was touch and go, with the tide of the battle shifting back and forth. What Joshua didn't know was that the ground where he and his chosen men were fighting was not the primary battlefield. Another more crucial fight—an unseen battle—was occurring on top of the nearby hill.

Before Joshua took to the battlefield, Moses told him, "I will stand on top of the hill with the staff of God in my hands" (Ex. 17:9). What's the significance of that? It meant that Moses would be praying. He would be interceding with God on behalf of Joshua and the men fighting alongside him.

As the Israelites fought, Moses prayed, and God was answering his prayer. But when Moses grew weary and let his hands drop to his sides, the Amalekites gained the upper hand. When Moses raised his hands back up, the battle turned. "As long as Moses held up his hands, the Israelites were winning, but whenever he lowered his hands, the Amalekites were winning" (v. 11).

I wonder how long it took for Moses to figure this out. Did he notice it first or did Aaron or Hur, the men who went to the top of the hill with him? Did they have a hard time believing their eyes? Did they wonder how a real-world physical battle could be controlled by the hands-up battle of prayer? We know somebody figured it out, because the passage says, "When Moses' hands grew tired, they took a stone and put it under him and he sat on it. Aaron and Hur held his hands up—one on one side, one on the other—so that his hands remained steady till sunset" (v. 12).

No Passive Onlookers

No one who is married can afford to miss this. Prayer was not supplemental to winning the battle; it was instrumental. Too often we see prayer as passive, but it's not. It's vital. It's foundational. It's as critical to victory as Joshua and the fighters on the battlefield. Moses recognized there would be no victory unless he contended in hands-up prayer.

If you look at how Moses lived after this, you realize he carried this revolutionary belief—and practice—with him for the rest of his days. He knew that ultimately there could be no victory anywhere in life unless he stayed connected to God in prayer. You could say he lived the rest of his life with his hands up. When he climbed Mount Sinai to receive the Ten Commandments from God, I wonder if he physically raised his hands in prayer. And when he pitched the tent of meeting outside of camp and met with God, and "the LORD would speak to Moses face to face, as one speaks to a friend" (Ex. 33:11), did he feel compelled to put his hands up, remembering how God had fought for them against the Amalekites? We know Moses surrendered to God and relied on him. He once told God, "If your Presence does not go with us, do not send us up from here" (Ex. 33:15).

Prayer isn't something nice to do if you have time for it. If you want to have a long and happy marriage, it is *more* than half the battle. The question

> Prayer isn't something nice to do if you have time for it. If you want to have a long and happy marriage, it is *more* than half the battle.

is, Have you figured out what Moses did yet? Have you awakened to the reality that when it comes to prayer, you were never meant to be a passive onlooker? If you want to win in your marriage the way Moses and Joshua won in their battle, prayer isn't optional. It's a necessity. It's life or death! Prayer was the only hope for Moses. It was the only hope for Brian and Rachel. It was the only hope for Marcia and me. And it is the only hope for you.

Heroes of the Faith Got It

The great men and women of faith whose stories are told in the Bible understood that God's power was the answer to life's challenges. One of the greatest people who remained dependent on God was David, the warrior king of Israel. Psalm 33 is not attributed to a specific author, but many scholars believe David wrote it. It says, "No king succeeds with a big army alone, no warrior wins by brute strength. Horsepower is not the answer; no one gets by on muscle alone" (vv. 16–17 THE MESSAGE). David went to battle as Joshua did. But he also prayed with his hands up, the way Moses did. He knew his hard-fought victories came mostly by the Lord's hand.

I love that *The Message* uses the term *horsepower*. I told you in the previous practice that I'm a car guy. More specifically, I'm a Corvette guy. As I write this in 2020, the new midengine C8 Corvette is arriving. The base model has 490 horsepower. Imagine getting 490 horses harnessed up to your chariot and saying, "Giddy up!" That doesn't even make sense to us—490 horses harnessed together. As Jerry Seinfeld said in one of his stand-up routines, "Why do we even use the term *horsepower*? Is that to further humiliate horses? The space shuttle rockets have 20 million horsepower."[1] Measuring rocket power using horses doesn't make sense. How would you harness together a third of all the horses on the planet?[2] But you get the point. In David's day, horses were used in warfare.

Psalm 33 concludes this way:

> We wait in hope for the LORD;
>> he is our *help* and our *shield*.
> In him our hearts rejoice,
>> for we trust in his holy name.
> May your unfailing love be with us, LORD,
>> even as we put our hope in you.
> (vv. 20–22, emphasis added)

David knew where his help came from, and he understood prayer. He always asked God to fight for him, because he knew that without God he wasn't going to win his battles. Neither will we.

Battlefield Lessons

If the way prayer works has never made sense to you, then this is going to be one of the most significant breakthroughs you'll experience for your marriage. Or if you once knew the power of prayer but have lost your way, then being reminded of this and having your fire reignited will transform you. Or if you are already deeply connected to God in prayer, then this is going to add more fuel to your fire. The presence of God that comes from hands-up prayer releases the power of God in our lives, and that especially includes our marriages.

What lessons can we learn from Moses and Joshua that each of us can take into the fight to keep our marriages strong, healthy, and happy?

1. BECOME WARRIORS WHO FIGHT FOR YOUR MARRIAGE

God was with the Israelites, but they had to fight. Joshua was required to go down onto the battlefield, and he and his fellow warriors couldn't just show up and do nothing. They couldn't phone it in. They had to give their best, putting their energy and skills—limited as they were—into the fight in an attempt to win.

Marriage requires the same. You have to do the work of building a strong, healthy, happy marriage. You can't expect marriage to work unless you work at it. You need to develop skills, put them into practice, and work together to build the relationship. Ask yourself, Are you willing to fight for your marriage? Are you willing to do what it takes? If you can't definitively answer yes to these questions, then ask God to help you regain the will to fight. He'll help you if you ask.

2. BUT REMEMBER PRAYER IS MORE THAN HALF THE BATTLE

You must fight for your marriage. But while you fight, you also have to pray. Joshua, a novice commander facing a ruthless and experienced fighting force in the Amalekites, won because of prayer. There will never be enough marriage books, counseling sessions, good conversations, personality profiles, love language lessons, or gripe sessions with friends to compensate for a prayerless marriage. Never forget that more than 51 percent of the battle is in the supernatural realm. The power of God—accessed through surrendered prayer—is what ultimately tips the balance in the battle.

When you read the Bible from Genesis to Revelation, you'll find one theme that is stronger than any other for success in any endeavor: utter dependence on God. That's where people gain horsepower greater than their own to accomplish what's beyond their capability. When people are in over their heads, asking God for help is the answer. And in case you haven't figured it out yet, in marriage you are in over your head. You have to deal with anger, malice, lust, self-indulgence, emotional wounds, betrayal, disappointment, harsh words, covetousness, bitterness, sexual temptation, financial disagreement, keeping a record of wrongs, spite, impatience, overspending, underearning, worry, depression, health issues, parenting dilemmas, calendar pressures, economic hardship, hard-heartedness, and so on. Are you getting the idea? The marriage battlefield is filled with these challenges and more. There are times your spouse can feel more like an enemy against you than a fellow warrior facing the storms of life with you.

> There will never be enough books, counseling, or lessons to compensate for a prayerless marriage.

If you are going to have any hope for real happiness, you need horsepower greater than your own. You need the power of God to mature you to a level that is beyond you. How else can you develop a marriage filled with grace, patience, wisdom, understanding, faithfulness, joy, kindness, forgiveness, and self-discipline? In a successful marriage, you must become quick to listen, slow to speak, and slow to anger. You need to learn to resolve conflict. It's no small challenge to get two self-centered people to work together.

3. AND DON'T EXPECT KEEPING YOUR HANDS UP TO BE EASY

If you're wondering why more couples don't make prayer a central part of their marriage, it's because prayer is demanding. Even Moses found it difficult to keep his hands up. Why do you think the story of Moses on the hill praying with his hands up was included in the Bible? Was it so that Joshua, Israel, and every reader of the Bible would have a picture of prayer to learn from? Maybe. I'm not sure why God did a lot of the things recorded in the Bible. But I do know that prayer was a vital part of life for every person who walked with God, from Abraham to Moses to David to Jesus to the twelve disciples to members of the early church. And nothing in the Bible indicates anyone found it easy.

In a natural world that is unattuned to the supernatural realm, prayer can feel unnatural and tiring. In the busyness of life, it's easy to believe prayer is irrelevant. As we experience the demands of business, career, finances, parenting, calendars, taxiing the kids, to-do lists, health concerns, relational challenges, political unrest, and putting food on the table, we may think, *Who has time to pray? Leave that to spiritual people. Pastors have time for that. And Moses.* But that way of thinking is a mistake.

When Joshua went into battle, he may have believed he was doing the heavy lifting. He may have thought, *Hey, you three up on the hill, get down here with a sword and help us fight the battle!* But Moses *was* fighting the battle. What he was doing wasn't easy or safe. Even if Joshua hadn't yet figured it out, Moses understood that the natural and supernatural worlds operated together. He knew prayerlessness would cost them the victory, and that giving in to weariness would be the end of them.

Have you figured it out? Do you understand what's at stake if you don't pray? If your hands are down, how can you hope for the power of God in your marriage? To put it in a more positive way, what could happen if you began to practice hands-up prayer for your marriage? When you really understand that the victory you seek in marriage is dependent on prayer, you will find a way—you will *make* a way—to pray. You will carve out time to pray at all costs, even if it means turning off Netflix or getting up early in the morning or setting aside a hobby.

How God Improves a Marriage

So how does prayer help? How does God work to make a marriage better? Recently I was talking about this with Chris Morgan, a good friend who is a worship leader and prayer warrior. He and I have worked together for a couple of decades and know each other very well. He recounted a season of his life where God turned things around in his marriage because he put his hands up in prayer.

The nature of marriage is that it humbles you. It draws out conflicts between two people who love each other but can drive each other crazy. My wife, MaryAnn, and I seemed to be doing as well as anyone, but somewhere around twenty years into our marriage, the wheels started falling off.

Nobody wants to be in a miserable marriage, including me. So I was reading books about marriage to try to figure out how to fix things. But what was more important was that the misery I was experiencing became a diving board into conversations with God. For about a year to eighteen months, I found myself in a long journey of prayer. Honestly, I'm not sure I would have ever entered that kind of intensive prayer without the kind of breakdown MaryAnn and I were experiencing. But curiously, God began to reveal to me things I had been doing for a long time that were causing the breakdown in my marriage.

God had the wisdom I needed, and only the desperation I felt in my marriage prompted me to seek the answers only God could provide through prayer. In that context, God used a conversation with a friend to reveal to me that I was more truth-based than love-based in my marriage. As the better arguer, I would prove my view as true. But while I was winning arguments in my mind, I was losing MaryAnn's heart in my marriage. I had pushed her into a no-win corner, and she was just reacting to it.

While God was revealing these things to me on long walks of prayer, he was also repairing me through prayer. He revealed that I was sabotaging the very relationship I was begging him to fix. It was arresting. My misery in marriage drove me to prayer. Prayer changed me. And as I changed, God changed our marriage.

At the end of that two-year period, I looked up and realized we had a better marriage. God had used prayer as a powerful tool to refine me from the inside out. Ever since, prayer has been how I love my wife. It's how I remain surrendered to God and attentive to my marriage. I haven't ceased being a philosophy major with a bent toward telling prophetic-type truth. But now I'm aware of what's wrong when I fall into old bad habits. Prayer corrects negative drift in my marriage.

Chris described the pattern God often uses to fix marriages. We start to pray. Maybe we're not good at it and aren't even sure what exactly to ask for, other than God's intervention. We ask God to fix our marriage or our spouse. And we start talking to God. That opens us up to God more than we were before. God gives us extra horsepower when we're exhausted and ready to give up. (In case you haven't figured it out, that God-given horsepower is what helps us endure the B Zone when all we want to do is go to the Q Zone.) As we continue praying, God shows us where we're falling short. But he doesn't leave us there; he helps us. And when we're willing, he starts to change us. He changes the way we think about our spouse. He helps us stop the negative behaviors that are undermining our relationship. He gives us grace, which makes it possible for us to give more grace to others, including our spouse. The relationship starts to improve. If our spouse is praying, God does the same with them. And eventually, we get on a better, healthier, happier path together.

How to Pray

Learning to practice hands-up prayer has helped shape our marriage. But unlike Chris and MaryAnn, Marcia and I didn't experience twenty smooth years out of the gate. As we've explained, we started with struggles. But we both built personal prayer lives and discovered that prayer was a crucial part of improving our marriage.

We encourage you to step out beyond whatever awkwardness you may feel and pray with your spouse. Don't overcomplicate it. Just talk to God together. Often, when Marcia and I crawl into bed for the night, I'll grab her hand or we'll spoon—yeah, I said that— and I'll just start praying. I usually thank God for parts of our day. I'll ask for God's help with our kids or career stuff. I'll pray for what's concerning Marcia or pray encouragement over her. It takes no more than three minutes. Usually she offers a brief prayer as well. We end with, "Give us good sleep. See you in the morning, Lord."

Don't just talk about praying. Do it. Pray however you can. The most difficult moment will be the first time you try it. Yes, it may be awkward. Don't let that stop you from praying again. Pray together seven consecutive days, and it will stop feeling quite so weird. And here's the great news: you'll draw closer to each other because you can't maintain distance for any length of time from someone you pray with and pray for. God will use the simple practice of praying together to knit the supernatural into your natural world.

> Don't just talk about praying. Do it.

In addition to praying with your spouse, keep talking to God on your own. If you're looking for specific help praying for your spouse, you can use the old faithful ACTS pattern, which is traditionally taught as adoration, confession, thanksgiving, and supplication.

ADORATION

Start by reading something from the Bible, like a psalm or a chapter in John's gospel, and allow it to bring you to a place where you acknowledge God's greatness. Or you might want to listen to, or sing along with, some worship music. (I only do this when I'm alone. Nobody but God wants to hear me sing.)

Not only is adoration God's due, it rightsizes our perspective. It helps us to have a more loving and grace-giving understanding of our spouse because of the love and grace God gives us. And it helps us to acknowledge that God is God, he loves us, and he can handle anything we throw at him, including our marriage problems.

CONFESSION

Once you've acknowledged God for who he is, it's time to get honest with God about where you're falling short. When I do this, I often reflect on the previous day. I ask God if there's sin I've committed that needs forgiving. If I possess an attitude or have taken an action that is displeasing to him, I ask for his forgiveness.

As you do this, particularly examine your relationship with your spouse. When I do this, I ask myself, "How did I think about Marcia? How did I treat her? How have I spoken to her or responded to her in the last twenty-four hours?" Trust me, there were many days when I had to go back to Marcia and say, "I'm sorry about my response yesterday," especially in years five through fifteen of our marriage. My confession was often met with something like, "Yeah, you didn't handle that very well."

Do you know how I wanted to answer? "Oh yeah? Well here's what you did!" But the appropriate response was another "I'm sorry," without explanation or excuses. I had to mature into that.

I need to point out something here. When God reveals something we've done that seems little, we should never dismiss or minimize it. Humbling ourselves, going to our spouse, and apologizing for small things can start to make big changes in us. That action shapes us and our marriages. When Chris Morgan realized what he was doing to MaryAnn, it wasn't enough for him to regret what he did. He needed to go to her, apologize to her, and change what he was doing, which was possible with God's help. That obedience to God's prompt made a difference and started the healing process.

As you pray, God may reveal your passive-aggressive behavior or how you're undermining your spouse in some way. Actions such as a snide remark, hurtful sarcasm, insincerity, rolling your eyes, ignoring their words, minimizing their feelings, escaping into entertainment, leaving the room, or going to bed early in silence are all little things that are hurtful to your spouse. When you ask in prayer, "Lord, is there anything I need to confess or change? Is there anything I'm doing that's sabotaging my marriage?" the Spirit of God will reveal them, and that can be painful. No wonder people quit praying!

If your spouse is doing the same thing in prayer time, it has a powerful impact on shaping your relationship. But even if you have to go it alone in prayer, do it. God will improve you, and the changes in you will be a peace offering to your spouse, and it will open the door for a better relationship.

THANKSGIVING

A spirit of ingratitude hurts marriages. Discontentment and angst within us often leak out in unkind ways toward our spouse and others. What's a good antidote to that? Thanksgiving. Few things improve a person's attitude better than gratitude. And let's face it; God deserves a lot of gratitude for all he has done for us and given to us.

When I get to this part of my prayer time, I try to get very specific about what I'm grateful for. And that list always includes Marcia. I focus on her best attributes and all the ways she loves and serves me, our children, and our grandchildren. And let me say one more thing. Our coauthor, Charlie Wetzel, often gives this piece of advice to the men he mentors: learn to love the person God has given you. Before you were married, you may have looked for particular attributes, personality traits, or physical features in the opposite sex. That's fine while you were dating. Now that you're married, learn to love the best traits your spouse possesses, and stop looking for what you don't have. Learn to celebrate who your spouse is.

STUFF (OR SUPPLICATION)

When I learned ACTS as a kid, the *S* stood for supplication. That's too complicated a word for me, so now I just think of it as stuff. Everybody has stuff to ask for. I usually pray through my calendar for the coming day. The stuff I ask God for is wisdom, help, and favor in the day's work. I pray over finances, decisions, health issues—the everyday battles of life. And I always include Marcia in these prayers. Her well-being and success are as important to me as mine.

You don't have to pray using ACTS. You may already have a way to pray that works for you. But I want to give you a piece of advice. Most of us do our prayer time backward. We want to start by focusing on our stuff, but then we often fail to do anything else. Then we dash off and start our day. We miss so much of the deep experience God offers when we do this. We are so much better off when we begin with hands-up prayer focused on God. Why? Because we experience more of his presence when we focus on him. We become humbler and more teachable. We actually want to confess our sins. We feel gratitude for God's grace, which fuels us to give others grace. As we focus on how big God really is, our problems get smaller in our eyes. We become more grateful, which makes thanksgiving a natural byproduct. By the time we get to our stuff, we have a healthier disposition. This process better prepares us to face our day. We know God is with us in the battle, just as Moses and Joshua did.

How often should you set aside a time to put your hands up and pray? Most of us have daily rhythms, so we need to pray daily. It is as essential to our spirits and our marriage relationship as food is for our bodies. Do we literally put our hands up when we pray? It's

> As we focus on how big God really is, our problems get smaller in our eyes.

not necessary, but many times that is exactly what I do. Not for my whole prayer time. I'm no Moses. But I often do literally raise my hands in prayer like Moses when I get to my stuff list, especially on days when I'm anticipating heavy battles. I even imagine myself on the hill overlooking the battle that we'll be fighting, be it for our marriage, finances, work, parenting, or health. It helps me focus.

I don't think that physical posture is required to engage in hands-up prayer, but if it helps, go for it. Prayer is the point. Get into whatever posture helps you to surrender and talk to your heavenly Father.

Marriage Breakthroughs

As Marcia and I recall the many breakthroughs and advances that we've made in our thirty-seven years of marriage, we recognize that nearly all of them have come as the result of hands-up prayer. In fact, most of the practices we're sharing in this book came from things we learned in prayer in direct response to specific problems we faced. Let us give you two examples.

The first occurred about eight years into our marriage. After a lot of challenges, Marcia and I at long last began to get above water financially and emotionally. On top of that, the church was finally growing after years of struggle. (If you want to know more about those challenges, you can read about them in my book *Home Run*.[3]) The church moved from rented space into our first facility. For the first time, I hired staff. It felt like I could finally breathe. But even though we were experiencing a pretty good place in our marriage, one issue kept recurring, which we'll explain in detail in practice 4. Because of it, we were stuck. When it started to color everything negatively, we went to a marriage counselor for the first time, but it didn't resolve our problem. Do you know what did? Praying. That led us to discover practice 4 in this book: take a knee or two.

The second happened about ten years into our marriage. We grew so weary of fighting each other that we had to ask God for help. We often treated each other like enemies. Our prayers led us to create what we call fair-fight rules and develop another one of the practices in this book: pick a fair fight (practice 3). Prayer was not what led us to discover the rules, but it has become a vital part of how we fight fair to resolve conflict.

Prayer has won many battles for us, and it has allowed God to teach us many lessons. Sometimes those lessons have come quickly. Other times they've taken longer, and both of us have had to work diligently to learn them. Occasionally, just one of us is in the battle, like Joshua, and the only thing the other can do is put up their hands and pray like Moses. That was the case for us in a battle Marcia fought for over a decade.

MARCIA: About thirteen years ago I began to develop some pretty debilitating physical issues: joint pain and high fevers followed by chills. We later found out there was swelling in my internal organs. Doctors ruled out rheumatoid arthritis, but they were baffled. At first, my symptoms would come and go, but eventually I had to live with constant fevers and exhaustion. This went on for months.

Even though I put on a brave face publicly and gutted out my duties as a wife, mother, and pastor's wife, I couldn't hide it from my family. They all experienced my illness, with Kevin having the clearest picture. He would come home to find me in bed or bundled up in blankets, barely able to function. You can imagine how frustrating and difficult it was for us. No answers and no way to make it better. There was nothing he could do to help, and there was no quick, easy fix.

KEVIN: If you were sitting here with me right now, you would see my tears as I write these words. Marcia and I never talked about this publicly. Until recently, the church had no knowledge about this part of our marriage journey. I watched Marcia crumble under the physical symptoms for more than a year's worth of doctors' appointments with no answers.

I'd climb the hill, so to speak, and pray, but the battle would just rage on. I begged God for understanding, yet none came. I was powerless to help Marcia, and it was undoing me emotionally. She was powerless to help herself, and it was undoing her as well. Every day I came home to emotional angst.

At the time, we had all four kids at home: a seventeen-year-old, a fifteen-year-old, a twelve-year-old, and a three-year-old. We were taking the biggest risks of our ministry career by building a twenty-four-hundred-seat worship center and launching into multicampus ministry for the first time. I was exhausted by work, and on top of that, my marriage partner was often physically and emotionally absent, though not by choice. To be brutally honest, I felt as bad for me as I did for her. It seemed like she was in quicksand, and I felt as if I were being dragged down with her. The only thing I could do about it was put my hands up in surrendered prayer.

MARCIA: We offered so many prayers during this time. Even though they didn't seem like they were being answered, I relied on what I knew about God: he is good, he loves me, and he has a plan. It was a season of tenacity and determination.

After three long years of hands-up prayer, we finally got a glimpse of light at the end of this dark tunnel. A gastroenterologist did a test that showed I had enlarged blood vessels. This prompted him to send me to a rheumatologist, who finally figured out what was going on. I didn't have rheumatoid arthritis, but I did have a rheumatic condition called adult Still's disease. After suffering for three years, I finally had a correct diagnosis. The rheumatologist prescribed a medication to control my symptoms. It was expensive, and it required me to give myself a shot every week. But it allowed me to function!

So, for most of the last decade, I have been on this very expensive and unpleasant regimen that has kept my symptoms at bay. And I'm grateful.

KEVIN: I'm grateful Marcia's debilitating health problems are in the past, that God answered our prayers to restore her to health through medication. For years now, Marcia has been strong and her old self again, which includes regular running and competing in races, including the occasional marathon.

What's amazing is that God is continuing to work in her and us in this journey as we continue to pray. A few months ago Marcia felt compelled to ask God for a complete healing from adult Still's, and she sensed that God had done it, so much so that she talked about getting off of her medication. In all honesty that scared me, because I didn't want her to suffer again the way she had. And I didn't want it to throw our life back into chaos.

So I went to God, raised my hands, and prayed. And after both of us spent time with the Lord, talking about it with him, she stopped taking her injections. And trust me, we celebrated in a big way when she experienced no negative side effects or symptoms. It appeared that God had healed her!

But I have to admit I wasn't feeling confident when she decided she wanted to run the Dopey Challenge at Walt Disney World. It's named for one of Snow White's seven dwarves, but do you know the real reason they call it that? Because you have to be dopey to do it. Over four consecutive days, participants run four races: a 5K, a 10K, a half-marathon, and a full marathon. Marcia's tough and strong, but I was worried it would cause a setback in her health.

MARCIA: I felt certain God had healed me, and I really wanted to take on the Dopey Challenge. So Kevin and I prayed about it, and we were in agreement before I tried it. And God was faithful. I completed all four races! It was exhausting and exhilarating. I'm glad I did it, but I won't ever be doing it again!

I believe the vast majority of us have battles similar

to the ones I've had. We often choose to keep them to ourselves, maybe because they are too intimate to share with others. But we need to share them with God. We need to raise our hands in prayer to him. Our experience helped us learn more about depending on God, and we both became stronger because of it.

When it comes to marriage, only you know the depth of the issues you're facing. And you may be the only person who understands the weaknesses and vulnerabilities of your spouse. Kevin prayed me through mine. And I pray him through his. We stand on the hill for each other. If you don't pray for your spouse, who will? The best way to help protect them is through your prayers. Hands-up, unceasing prayer.

KEVIN: That's not dopey, is it? It's another reminder that God invites us to engage in hands-up prayer. And he will provide as we prevail in prayer.

Like all couples, Marcia and I have faced our share of battles. We've faced battles since her health problems and, to be sure, we will face more. That's a normal part of marriage—and life. But God has always fought for us when we asked him to. When we put up our hands in surrender to him *and* fight for one another, we're doing all we can. We are taking down the wall between the natural and supernatural worlds in a way that invites God to bless us. The timing of his answers doesn't always match our expectations, and the outcome isn't always what we want, but it always is in our best interest and makes us better people. And happier.

So here are the most important questions of this practice. Are you fighting battles right now? Do you want to win them? What might God do in your marriage if you were to put your hands up, surrender to him, and ask for his help? Are you willing to do it? I can't guarantee what will happen, but I do guarantee that it will improve your marriage.

CONVERSATION FOR A COUPLE

Answer these questions on your own, with your spouse doing the same. Then make an appointment with each other to discuss your answers. Have an honest conversation with the goal of serving each other in order to develop a better marriage. Be honest with your feelings, but focus on how *you* can change by applying the practice described to yourself, not your spouse.

1. How would you describe your attitude toward prayer up to now? What is the single greatest obstacle you must over-come to engage in hands-up prayer?

2. In your eyes, what is the greatest barrier to praying with your spouse? What can *you* do to overcome your reluctance?

3. What challenge or problem are you facing *together* in your marriage that you would like your spouse to pray about?

4. What personal challenge or problem of *yours* would you like your spouse to pray about for you?

Once you've shared your answers, discuss what each of you needs to do as a result of your conversation.

| DISCUSSION FOR A SMALL GROUP |

1. What do you consider to be one of your greatest accomplishments? It can be in any area of life: athletic, professional, personal, relational, spiritual. Who helped you accomplish it?

2. Before reading this practice, what was your opinion about the interplay between the natural and supernatural worlds? What is your opinion now? Do you think these two worlds still interact today the same way they did in the time of Moses and Joshua? Explain.

3. What is your personal experience with prayer? Describe it.

4. Why do you think the image of having *hands up* was used? What is the significance? How can you apply it to your prayer life?

5. How difficult do you find it to pray for your spouse? How about *with* your spouse? What are the challenges for each?

6. What do you hope will change in your marriage by praying with and for each other?

7. What lesson or practice can you adopt as your own in prayer? How will you apply it?

8. Are you willing to commit to praying for each other and together for ten consecutive days? When, where, and how will you do it? Who will you ask to hold you accountable?

PRACTICE 3

Pick a Fair Fight

MMA (mixed martial arts) is big these days. So big, in fact, it's been called the fastest-growing sport on earth.[1] But in the mid-1960s when I was growing up, boxing was big. And the biggest name in boxing was Muhammad Ali. I have to admit, I've never been a big fan of boxing—to each his own—but like just about everyone back then, I knew about Muhammad Ali.

Why do I bring this up? Because during the time Ali was fighting, I had my first big boxing match. I was midway through kindergarten, and our family had moved. Our new house was a tiny rental—nine hundred square feet with one bathroom for a family of six. It was nothing much to look at. It was the only house in the entire neighborhood that didn't have a concrete driveway. It was gravel, if that tells you anything about the quality of the place and our economic situation. My two older brothers and I were jammed into a ten-by-eleven-foot bedroom. Our sister, even though she was the youngest, got a bedroom to herself. We thought the message was clear: girls are more important than boys.

Across the street lived Tommy, a boy who was a year older than I was, but who was still in kindergarten. He was my first big opponent. There were no gloves, no boxing ring, no referee, no bell, and no timer. It wasn't sanctioned, and there was no belt on the line. It was your typical neighborhood scrap. As I recall, the fight started when Tommy called me short and pushed me. I wasn't going to take that. My response to Tommy? I pushed him back and called him a dunce. The fight was on!

Now, it wasn't a fair fight, because I was not in Tommy's weight class; he was about twice my size. By all accounts he won the fight, since I was the one who ended up with the bloody nose. But even at age five, I knew instinctively that I had won the war. Why? I had bloodied his ego by fighting back fiercely instead of backing down. And while my physical bruises healed, he had a harder time healing from his psychological bruises. Even though we fought, or maybe because we did, we became best friends.

Growing up, I was a fighter. I would get into it with my two brothers, who were older and bigger. And like with Tommy, I learned I had to stand up for myself. I usually wasn't the one who started a fight, but I was always ready to finish one.

Unfortunately, I took that attitude into my marriage.

Marcia and I have already told you about our grocery store argument. That was only one of dozens—maybe hundreds—of verbal battles we had in the first decade of marriage. These conflicts never got physical, but we definitely hit each other below the belt verbally in our efforts to win. It wasn't pretty or kind or honoring.

Up and Down

Of course, our relationship wasn't all bad. We weren't always fighting. There were plenty of fun moments and lots of humor. A few years after Marcia and I planted 12Stone Church, one of the people who visited the church was a single guy named Barry. According to the person who invited him, Barry came to the church with a dual purpose: he wanted to play softball, and he wanted to find a wife. We were in alignment with goal number one. We had a softball team, and we were glad to have another good player on the roster. But his second goal? I wasn't sure about the wisdom of picking a struggling start-up church that met in rented space with only eighty people—most of whom were married couples with kids. Our church did not seem like a great place for a young guy to shop for a spouse. But we welcomed Barry and were glad to have him.

Barry loves to tell the story of the day he was checking out the women in the congregation and perked up when he spotted a beautiful young woman.

"Hey," Barry asked the friend who invited him, "what about that gal over there?"

"*Barry!*" his friend responded. "That's the *pastor's* wife!" He was looking at Marcia.

Barry didn't hesitate. "Well, are they getting along?"

We still laugh at that story. And it has a happy ending because Barry did find his wife, Casey, at our little church. They have been married for over twenty-five years and have been major players at the church.

Today, Casey and Marcia are good friends and running buddies.

When Marcia did the Dopey Challenge, Casey did it with her. But the truth is that back when Barry asked whether Marcia and I were getting along, the answer would have been both yes and no. We were putting a good face on our relationship publicly, but we were fighting all the time. Couples who fight like we did often end up sleeping in separate bedrooms. It never came to that, but the sex and the positive times weren't ever going to fix our ongoing problems. We had to find a way to deal with our issues.

What Are You Going to Do with Conflict?

Conflict in any marriage is inevitable. It's impossible to agree on everything with your spouse because you're two different individuals. How you deal with that conflict will determine the health and length of your marriage. You can pretend the conflict doesn't exist and let it eat at you internally. You can become passive-aggressive, never really dealing with the problems or resolving them, creating a tense environment. You can get into verbal or physical brawls that create emotional and relational damage. Or you can do what Marcia and I eventually did: learn to fight fair.

Have you ever thought about the idea of a fair fight in marriage? In regular life, there are different kinds of fights. In an alleyway or on a battlefield, people may have to literally fight for their lives. In those situations, there are no rules. It's a matter of survival. However, it's also true that some people voluntarily agree to step into a ring or an octagon to face an opponent in an official contest.

Those fights are planned, and they are designed to be fair. The two opponents agree to face each other. The event is scheduled, with the time and place mutually agreed upon. The fight has boundaries and specific rules. A referee makes sure the participants follow those rules. There is a reward of money or a trophy or a belt at the end. And the winner gets their hand raised in front of a cheering crowd.

This kind of fight became our inspiration. What if Marcia and I could pick a *fair* fight? What if we could set up some boundaries—some fair-fight rules—and follow them to resolve our conflict? And what if instead of one person's hand being raised in victory at the other's expense, we could finish with *both* of our hands raised in victory?

Let's face it: in marriage, there's really no way for one person to win and the other to lose without the marriage itself losing. If we could learn to fight *together* toward a common resolution—without name-calling, bloody noses, or verbal hits below the belt—it would change our relationship. The outcome would be a winning *marriage*, with the ultimate trophies being silver, golden, and maybe even diamond wedding anniversaries. We could choose a long and rewarding marriage instead of a life of conflict and misery!

So, in our late twenties, Marcia and I wrote what we call our fair-fight rules. Once we figured them out and agreed to them, they became like a subcontract of our marriage vows, a practical expression of our promise to love and honor 'til death do us

> In marriage, there's really no way for one person to win and the other to lose without the marriage itself losing.

part. These rules were our agreement to pursue open and honest communication. We want to teach them to you.

Are you ready to rumble in a positive way? If so, prepare to learn how to go twelve rounds, divided into three stages:

- Stage 1: Four rounds of communication
- Stage 2: Four rounds of compromise
- Stage 3: Four rounds of (optional) counseling

When conflict arises, and Marcia or I are angry, resentful, hurt, or disgruntled, this process is what we turn to. It works for us, and it can work equally well for you.

Prefight Rules

Before we get into the details of the rounds, it's important to lay the prefight ground rules. Without these, the process won't work. Marcia and I needed to abide by these eight rules to keep the fight fair.

1. PICK A FAIR FIGHT

Either member of a couple is free to call for a fair fight to address a problem or conflict, but the fight cannot happen when it's called. Instead, the fight has to be scheduled and agreed upon. Neither person is free to simply dive into an issue or interrupt what the other person is doing to try to resolve the conflict on the spot, just because they want to. Don't you hate it when you're in the middle of something, and your spouse just assumes you're free to have a conversation, especially a long, complicated, and negative one? Yeah, us too. So that's the first prefight rule. You have to call for a fight ahead of time. You can't just have a fair fight spontaneously— that would be a street brawl.

2. SUMMARIZE THE ISSUE

The person calling for the fair fight must summarize the issue to be discussed. This makes sure there is no intentional blindsiding at the time of the fight. It also gives a sense of how long the fight might take. That's important for the next rule. We'll give you an example of how that works later.

3. SCHEDULE THE FIGHT

Once a fair fight has been called, both parties are required to stop what they're doing right then and schedule a specific day and time to have the fight. Failing to do that is considered a violation of the rules. (See below for the penalty.) You need to work around kids (if you have them), plan for privacy, and find the right place. For us, scheduling had another consideration: we never planned for a fight to go past 11:00 p.m. Nothing constructive happens for us after that hour, because we usually run out of energy, get weary, become impatient, and lose the filter that stops us from trading harsh words. We can plan to start a fight at any time that works, but we always have a hard stop at 11:00. Everyone needs to figure out the time that works best for them.

4. SHOW UP AND FULLY ENGAGE

It is against the rules to miss a scheduled fight. (See below for the penalty.) Also, when the time starts, both parties are required to give their full, undivided attention to the other person and the conversation. No television, no phones, no computers, no distractions of any kind. Deep, honest, vulnerable conversation is possible only when both people are present and remain fully engaged.

5. KEEP THE FIGHT CLEAN

This is where it can get difficult. Once the fair fight begins, neither person is allowed to use harsh words or name-calling, say "you always" or "you never," or bring up old wounds or grievances to deflect the conversation or inflict pain. None of these actions is helpful. Couples need to respect each other's vulnerabilities. If they don't keep the fight clean, it's considered a violation of the rules. (Again, see below for the penalty.)

6. NEVER THROW IN THE TOWEL

Both people must agree to stay in the fight for every round, no matter how high the tension gets or how long it takes to complete. That means no storming off, no clamming up, no derailing the discussion. It also means not holding back any part of the problem. The couple needs to dig down to the last 10 percent of the issue. If another issue comes up during this fight that needs its own discussion, they should schedule a separate fair fight for that issue at another time.

Marcia and I always desire to bring our fight to a complete conclusion in that one session. It doesn't always happen, but that's the goal. If it needs all twelve rounds, so be it. If we run out of time but still haven't worked through the whole problem, we schedule a continuation.

7. FINISH THE FIGHT THE RIGHT WAY

Regardless of whether you finish the fight or schedule a continuation, the couple must do two things at the end of the session: say "I love you" and hug each other. A fair fight should never diminish a couple's love for each other. It should *increase* it. Take your cue from the MMA fighters. After two fighters have spent time beating up each other and the match is over, they often hug. Why? Because they respect each other. If they can do it, so can you!

8. PAY THE PRICE FOR BREAKING THE RULES

Okay, multiple times we've referenced the penalty for breaking the rules. It's the last rule: if a person violates one of the other rules, they must humble themselves before their spouse with a sincere spirit and apologize by saying, "You were right and I was wrong. You were right and I was wrong. You were right and I was wrong. I'm sorry. Will you please forgive me?" The wrongful party must do that for *each* violation. For us, that is a pretty stiff penalty, because neither of us likes to admit we're wrong. In response, the person receiving the apology must agree to forgive and move on.

> MARCIA: You know that three-peat apology? That was totally Kevin's idea. He *hates* to be wrong, and he knew the only thing that would prompt him to keep the rules was if he had a severe penalty. Saying "I'm sorry" three times is something he absolutely would not ever want to do.
>
> KEVIN: She's not kidding. You'll have to figure out what penalty works in your marriage.

MARCIA: Also, summarizing the nature of the issue is important so that we never blindside each other. That means, if I want to talk about the finances and budget, then I would have to put that on the table when I ask for the fair fight. And I have to be specific. For example, I might say, "Kevin, I call a fair fight. I want to discuss why it seems to me that you get to blow the budget. And since you control the checkbook, you can hide what you did, but I don't have that same freedom. That really makes me angry."

Do you see what I did there? I did not indict him with a *fact*. I picked a fair fight and expressed a *feeling*. It doesn't make what I'm feeling true, but it does mean that this is how I experienced it. We do *not* start the fight when I ask for the fair fight. We wait for the time when the fair fight is scheduled.

KEVIN: Exactly. Summarizing is not a time to vent. Marcia simply states her experience, and I don't respond to her summary by defending myself or giving my two cents. We just get out our iPhones and set a time. When the kids were young, it was usually right after they went to bed. And we have always avoided using our date night for a fair fight.

We set a time because it helps us avoid the venting and damage that is often done in the heat of the moment, where tensions can rise, emotions can run high, and self-restraint becomes low. Such behavior fuels conflict instead of ending it. Setting a time also gives us a chance to prepare, pray, invite God into the process, and think. I tend to think as I speak, but Marcia prefers to write out her thoughts in advance since she's less verbal.

MARCIA: I like that I can call for the fair fight about anything that is frustrating to me, ruining my peace of mind, or feeling unfair.

The great thing about fair fights is that if you agree to stick with the fair-fight rules, you can use them to address and resolve *anything*:

- "I don't like the way you handle money."
- "I think you're online too much."
- "How come you work too many hours?"
- "How come you hide from conflict?"
- "How come you drink so much?"
- "I feel like your bad temper is ruining our relationship. Why can't you stop?"
- "Why have all the household chores become mine to do all the time?"
- "Why don't we talk anymore?"
- "It feels like you care more about the kids than us."
- "How come you want so much sex?"
- "How come you want so little sex?"
- "Why won't you stop watching porn when you know it hurts me and our marriage?"
- "How come you are so attached to your parents?"
- "How come you never discipline the kids?"

- "Why won't you go to church with me?"
- "Why don't you spiritually lead our home?"

We could go on. Anything that's a conflict, problem, obstacle, or barrier for any couple can be the subject of a fair fight. You just need to pick it and schedule it.

Into the Ring

The eight prefight rules may feel a little complicated when you first read them, but they really are pretty simple. They made sense to us, and we hope they make sense to you. Why go to all that trouble? Because your goal is to pick a fair fight that comes to a *resolution*—a win-win, not a bloody brawl.

Once the stage is set with the prefight rules, the rounds are straightforward.

STAGE 1: COMMUNICATION (ROUNDS 1–4)

The first stage is really about listening and understanding. The couple's goal is to make sure they are on the same page and won't be working at cross-purposes. They will both know the subject, because that was stated when they scheduled the fight. Now it's time to understand each other's perspective.

Round 1: One person talks, explaining their perspective on the issue, using the tone suggested in Ephesians 4:15: "speaking the truth in love." The other person listens without interrupting, being inattentive, or acting defensively in word or action.

Our experience has taught us that regardless of who calls the fair fight, the less verbal person should go first. In our case, that's Marcia. Having the less verbal person *always* speak first helps balance out the interaction.

Round 2: The person who listened in round 1 must restate in their own words what they think the speaker said, communicating the heart of the message as well as the ideas. If the restating is correct, the speaker confirms they have been heard. If not, they repeat the process. Round 3 can't begin until the first speaker agrees that the listener got it.

Round 3: In round 3 they change roles. The listener from round 1 becomes the speaker, sharing their perspective on the issue. Again, the listener cannot interrupt, be inattentive, or act defensively—verbally or nonverbally.

Round 4: The listener in round 3 must restate in their own words what they think the speaker said, communicating the heart of the message as well as the ideas. If the restatement is correct, the speaker confirms they have been heard. If not, they repeat the process. They can't go to round 5 until the speaker agrees that the listener got it.

KEVIN: I'm a type A personality and Marcia is type B, so I'm better at arguing. We've found that my tendency is to try to overwhelm her, verbally dominate her, and convince her that I am right. That's why she *always* goes first.

MARCIA: Kevin can present a very convincing argument, but that doesn't automatically mean he's right. I really don't like to go first because I'm quieter and more introverted. Honestly, I would rather not speak at all when I'm angry. I'd rather give him the silent treatment. But that's not helpful. If I talk first, I start to let down my defenses, and I'm in a better place to know when to give in and when to stick up for myself. But my going first is not an easy rule for me. Not for either of us!

KEVIN: The purpose of the first four rounds is to change the way you listen. I confess that just because I can think fast and talk fast, that doesn't mean I can listen fast. The truth is, there's no such thing as listening fast.

It will take you some time to learn how to do the first four rounds well. Most people's natural instinct is to defend themselves or argue their perspective, not to listen and restate what the other person has said. Even seasoned marriage veterans can stumble when it comes to communication and listening skills. Our friends Corey and Bethany Baker, who have six children, told us a story of one of their interactions that had us howling in laughter. It illustrates the importance of being a good listener. Corey said,

I came home from work, and it had been a tough day with a lot of fires to put out and a lot going on. I got home and our kids were running around, and there was still a lot to do.

A few minutes later Bethany and I had a chance to catch up and give each other updates on some stuff. But it seemed like it was taking her a really long time to say what she wanted to say.

Without thinking, I did that hurry-up circular motion with my hand. And she just stopped and gave me a look.

"Baby, just land the plane," I said stupidly.

"Oh, it's landed," she said with an icy stare.

"Now don't get emotional," I said. "Just land the plane."

"Oh, it's landed," she snapped. "We're done." Then she turned and walked away.

I thought, *Note to self: don't ever tell my wife to land the plane. And second, don't add fuel to the fire by saying, "Don't get emotional."*

That was not one of my better days as a husband!

Corey is usually pretty good at communication; he's actually a very high-level executive coach. But his story is a good reminder that *everyone* needs to work at becoming a better listener, especially with their spouse.

It's crucial to understand that there can never be a *fair* fight until you truly understand the other person with clarity and empathy. That's the whole purpose of stage 1. If you don't master listening and understanding, you won't be successful in stage 2.

STAGE 2: COMPROMISE (ROUNDS 5–8)

Once you have defined the issue from both perspectives, and you agree that you really understand each other, you can move forward to the next four rounds.

Round 5: The less verbal person offers their solution. They tell what they believe would help the couple and family achieve a win. The other person listens without interrupting.

Round 6: The more verbal person offers their solution. They tell what they believe would help the couple and family achieve a win. The other person listens without interrupting.

Round 7: Both people freely discuss possible solutions until they carve out an agreement. That means continuing the dialogue regardless of the emotional tension, without name-calling, harsh words, or temper tantrums, until they come to a compromise they both believe they can live with. If they reach their agreed-upon hard-stop time before reaching a compromise, they must schedule another fair-fight session to continue working to resolve the issue.

Round 8: If they successfully complete round 7 and come to a compromise, then they agree to pray about it until both feel enough peace that they can agree that the issue is resolved and they are willing to commit to it.

If you're like us, you might choose to write out the compromise in detail to ensure that there's no confusion about it later. We have even signed these written agreements to confirm our mutual commitment. We do this not because we lack trust but because it helps us build trust.

Once we agree to the compromise, we are mutually bound to honor our agreement. If one of us stumbles, they must self-correct and pay the price of a triple apology. The other person agrees to forgive in the spirit of Galatians 6:1: "If someone falls into sin, forgivingly restore him, saving your critical comments for yourself. *You* might be needing forgiveness before the day's out" (THE MESSAGE).

If both people can't get to a place of agreement, then they must repeat rounds 5 through 8 until they do. Or they can choose to go into the last stage: counseling.

The compromise round is how Marcia and I grew up and learned how to get along. If you chafe against the idea of compromise, then I'll share with you something my mentor John Maxwell said to me over lunch one day: "Anyone who says, 'There's no such thing as compromise,' has never been married."

We all come into marriage as idealists. During the honeymoon phase, love is blind, and we often don't see our differences. But at some point, as David Augsburger suggested in his book *Sustaining Love*, you move from idealism to disillusionment, and then all you can see are the differences.[2] That's where marriages often get stuck. When couples focus on each other's differences, they tend to get stuck, get stubborn, and dig in—unless they choose to compromise. It's the only way forward.

> When couples focus on each other's differences, they tend to get stuck, get stubborn, and dig in—unless they choose to compromise.

One area that has prompted multiple fair fights for Marcia and me relates to our schedule and calendar. During one of those fair fights, in round 1, Marcia said,

I want to talk about dinnertime. We have two kids and you come home anytime you want between five and seven at night. It feels like I cannot count on you for a specific time, the kids can't count on you, and a meal cannot be kept for you. It feels like we are always adjusting to your work, and your work is never adjusting to our family. I know your work is demanding, but I'm exasperated, and we need a real solution.

While she spoke, I listened and took some notes. And in round 2, I explained her feelings and perspective back to her. Once she agreed that I understood, I shared my perspective in round 3. I said,

> I'm a solo pastor of a church that is barely working. I have no one to cover for me when anyone in the church has a need. If I fail, we not only stumble in our calling for the kingdom, we go bankrupt personally. We have put our entire lives on the line, we have lost everything financially for this work, and I feel owned by it all. I'd love to have the freedom of sticking to a schedule, but how? How am I supposed to absorb the pressure of work with people in the congregation and the pressure of home from you without being torn apart?

She listened and repeated back what I had said, and then we moved on to rounds 5 through 8. We each empathized with the other's perspective. We realized that each of us experienced a specific pressure the other person didn't experience or fully appreciate. However, we both longed for a great marriage, a strong family, and solid kids. We also longed to lead a life-giving church. But we would not have a life-giving church if we did not have a great marriage, strong family, and solid kids. And you know what? We found a compromise that felt like a win for both of us.

I agreed to change my lifestyle. I went to work earlier in the morning to get the regular day-to-day work of the church done, and I scheduled my planned appointments to be finished by 5:00 p.m. That gave me thirty minutes of grace time to get home by 5:30, which I committed to do 90 percent of the time. And anytime I didn't arrive home by then, it had to be for a really good reason.

Pastors can't entirely avoid working evenings; it's part of the job. But I restricted my work to no more than three nights during any given week. And those nights were planned ahead of time. On the other four nights, I was home and able to put the kids to bed.

Believe it or not, this was a major shift in our marriage and family. Marcia was finally able to plan dinner and count on me to be home for family time. It forced me to learn how to manage my calendar and meetings. I was no longer casual in my attitude, assuming I could work late to get things done. I worked smarter and harder during the day. Our family dinners became meaningful times that shaped our family. Sure, we still had to work out our schedule for sports and other events, but everything changed after we both laid our perspectives on the table and started to work *with* each other rather than *against* each other.

Another time I asked for a fair fight about how we managed the tension between fair fights! I did that because it seemed like we were fine all during the week, but conflict kept hitting us on Saturdays. Then on Sunday morning, while I was trying to lead the church spiritually, I felt like Marcia was sitting in the front row with her arms crossed, glaring at me, thinking, "Really, Pastor? Like you have it all together!"

So I called for a fair fight to talk about it. We went through all the rounds, and we concluded in round 7 that the Devil wanted us to fight on Saturdays to prevent us from doing what God wanted on Sundays. Our compromise was to never let conflict arise on the weekend so we could focus on serving the people we love at 12Stone.

Maybe you're thinking, *Well, that's ridiculous.*

No, it's not. We both agreed that whenever we felt irritation, annoyance, selfishness, or anger on the weekend, each would own it as our own problem and submit to God, with James 4 as our guide:

> What causes fights and quarrels among you? Don't they come from your desires that battle within you? . . .
>
>> "God opposes the proud
>> but shows favor to the humble."
>
>> Submit yourselves, then, to God. Resist the devil, and he will flee from you. Come near to God and he will come near to you. . . . Humble yourselves before the Lord, and he will lift you up. (vv. 1, 6–8, 10)

Our compromise for the weekend was that neither of us got our way, but God got his.

We want to say one more thing about compromise. It's really about perspective. Marriage experts Les and Leslie Parrott have spoken at our church before. One weekend I interviewed them about compromise, and Les told me a story. They had started dating in high school and married young. Early in their relationship, Les asked Leslie to promise she would never drink coffee. Seriously. They both wanted to live a healthy lifestyle, and Les had seen his parents have a hard time getting going in the morning without coffee, so he didn't want either of them to drink it. That was important to him, so she promised.

But then at her first job, she became the one who made the coffee in the office, and she fell in love with it. Les got really worked up about it. He was annoyed about her need for coffee, the price of Starbucks, the whole thing. It caused a major rift in their marriage.

Then one day Les thought, *What are you doing? You won't compromise on* coffee? He realized how ridiculous that was. So he relented. Les said, "You don't always get your way in life, so finding that win-win and bending like a palm tree to compromise for your spouse is one of the great gifts and blessings you give each other."

Real love in real marriages requires real compromise. And here's the good news: when you pick a fair fight and go through the rounds, being honest with each other and really understanding each other, it becomes easier to find a compromise that you both think is fair and that works. And every time you both win, you become happier with each other and your relationship.

> Real love in real marriages requires real compromise.

STAGE 3: COUNSELING (OPTIONAL ROUNDS 9–12)

If you process through the eight rounds in stages 1 and 2, and you still can't find a compromise, then it's probably time to get some outside help.

Round 9: Both people make a list together of trusted friends they can each talk to about their issue. Then they talk to them separately to gain wisdom, insight, and perspective.

Round 10: The couple discuss what they learned from their friends and apply it to seek a compromise they can agree to. If they still can't resolve the issue, they move to round 11.

Round 11: They agree to meet with their pastor or a professional marriage counselor to gain wisdom, insight, and perspective on their issue.

Round 12: The couple discuss what they learned from their pastor or counselor, and they again work together to try to find a compromise.

Marcia and I have gone to rounds 9 and 10 quite a few times over the years. We've also been deadlocked and needed to go all the way to round 12. The most challenging time we had to do that taught us a lesson we discuss later in this book: take a knee or two (practice 4). We'll tell you the whole story when we get there, but for now I'll just say that, at the time, we paid more money than we could afford to get advice I did not want to solve an issue I wished Marcia would just give in on. That conflict sucked the joy out of our marriage for a season. It took three years to process and resolve, and picking a fair fight wasn't enough. We had to go to the Great Referee for that one. Some conflicts require a compromise that makes one person feel as if they didn't win. But in the end, it became a win for both of us.

If you can't find a compromise in stage 2 and have to enter stage 3, the people in round 9 may be enough to help you. Friends are some of the greatest gifts of God, particularly other couples who share your faith and strive to live a Christ-centered life of obedience, rooted in prayer. Getting perspective from friends who have no skin in the game helps. They may ask questions, share experiences of theirs, or offer advice that shifts your thinking. God often used friends to soften Marcia's will and mine and to counsel us toward a workable compromise. And we often benefited from their prayers for us.

Keep in mind that, in round 9, who you ask for advice and how you do it really matters. We talked only to people who were trustworthy and mature. We didn't choose anyone who was so loyal to one of us that they would automatically take that person's side, even if they were clearly wrong. We sought people who offered balanced advice. And we never picked an adviser who bashed their spouse. To be blunt, I believe anyone who bashes their spouse wouldn't be trustworthy handling my marriage issues, because I don't consider them to be trustworthy in handling their own issues. If someone disrespects their spouse verbally, they also disrespect their spouse in their heart, and that spirit of disrespect would poison their advice. We follow the advice of Paul, who said, "[Love] does not dishonor others, it is not self-seeking, it is not easily angered, it keeps no record of wrongs. . . . It always protects" (1 Cor. 13:5, 7).

We want to say one more thing about sharing with friends. Before you talk to them, both of you need to agree on what specific things you will share. Just as we honor sexual intimacy in our marriage by keeping appropriate things private, the same should be true with emotional intimacy. So whatever we process in our marriage relationship remains private unless we mutually agree to process it with friends. This is important for building mutual trust. Why? So we can be completely vulnerable and honest with each other without having to wonder if our spouse will later discuss it with friends.

Now, you might be thinking, *I should be able to say whatever I want with my friends when we're hanging out. It's how I process. I need to vent. It's my life, too, and that's how I tolerate being married. It shouldn't be up to my spouse to determine what I talk about.* Our response is that your first commitment is to your spouse. To have a deep, fulfilling, happy marriage, you need to build complete trust and have the freedom to be emotionally naked and honest with each other. It's the only way to have authentic emotional intimacy. For that reason, we never share our spouse's thoughts or perspective with others without permission. Our spouse approves what can be said and to whom.

Over time, picking a fair fight and following the rules will become natural to you. The right way to interact with each other when something is bothering you will become engrained in your thinking, and you will develop healthy instincts. Early on, Marcia and I had to use a fair-fight rules sheet we had created for ourselves. But eventually, when we had a conflict, we knew instinctively what to do. In time, it even became less important that Marcia speak first in every round 1. We no longer needed to write down our solutions or sign them. Fighting fairly so that we could both win changed our hearts and our habits. And that's huge when you consider where we started.

Pick Maturity over Harmony

Maybe you didn't start where Marcia and I did in our marriage, with below-the-belt verbal battles. Maybe you don't fight at all. If you're passive-aggressive, then we hope you know that's not a good thing, and you give our fair-fight rules a try. But what if you believe in keeping the peace so much that you choose harmony at all costs? We believe that is costing you more than you think.

A couple we know made this choice for many years in their marriage. When they got married a year out of college, they were very idealistic. "We will be poor, but it will be romantic," they said.

They were half-right. They were destitute, but it wasn't romantic. And it didn't take them long to turn on each other. After being married for only a few months, both of them were wishing for a way out.

When she became pregnant, they tried to make their marriage work. But their solution to their problems was to stuff them, because they were afraid that bringing up any differences would lead to a fight. For example, early in their marriage, he went out to eat all the time even though they couldn't afford it. While she was much more frugal in that area, she tended to buy décor items they couldn't afford for their apartment. Neither brought up their issues with the other, even though their habits were wrecking them financially.

As they swept their problems under the carpet and walked on eggshells around each other, what developed was a shallow harmony, the *appearance* that everything was fine. That gave them a false sense of peace. But their relationship couldn't develop the maturity that comes from working through problems together. That had to be earned.

Today, they are trying to find a better path forward. This means working to have the difficult conversations that lead to maturity, even when it means experiencing less harmony in the moment. Doing the hard work will ultimately lead to greater harmony in the long run. But you can't skip the process.

There is conflict in your marriage. How do we know that? Because you're married! If you want to experience the Second Happy in your marriage, you need to deal with that conflict. Commit to picking fair fights and become really good at resolving them so both of you can have your hands raised in victory at the end of the bout. Do that and you will earn maturity along with a deep and lasting harmony.

What's Even Better than a Fair Fight?

You may be wondering, *Will the fighting ever stop? Will we ever be able to stop calling for fair fights in our marriage?* Let us give you some hope. At this stage in our marriage, Marcia and I still have conflicts, but we rarely have to call for a fair fight anymore. We have solved so many conflicts together that we usually already know what we need to do to serve each other and create compromises. Now if something is bothering one of us, before we call for a fair fight, we take the issue to God in prayer. When I do that, I have a conversation with God with Philippians 2:3–8 in mind:

> Do nothing out of selfish ambition or vain conceit. Rather, in humility value others above yourselves, not looking to your own interests but each of you to the interests of the others.
>
> In your relationships with one another, have the same mind-set as Christ Jesus:
>
> Who, being in very nature God,
>> did not consider equality with God something to be used
>>> to his own advantage;
>
> rather, he made himself nothing
>> by taking the very nature of a servant,
>> being made in human likeness.
>
> And being found in appearance as a man,
>> he humbled himself
>> by becoming obedient to death—
>>> even death on a cross!

I've found that 95 percent of the time I want to call for a fair fight, it's because I'm not living according to Jesus's standard described in Philippians 2. Instead of planning a fight, I need to absorb the offense and move on, serve Marcia better and move on, or pray for Marcia and ask God to help her.

For the first twenty-five years of marriage, I wasn't mature enough to do this. Neither was Marcia. But it has happened in the last twelve years. It's a kind gift from God that we don't take for granted. Oh, I'll admit to a bit of angst and whining with the Lord. Getting over yourself is never easy. But in the end, marriage is an invitation to learn how to love the way Jesus does. The more we can die to self and become alive to God, the more our marriage becomes a candidate for God's favor and blessing.

> In the end, marriage is an invitation to learn how to love the way Jesus does.

CONVERSATION FOR A COUPLE

Answer these questions on your own, with your spouse doing the same. Then make an appointment with each other to discuss your answers. Have an honest conversation with the goal of serving each other in order to develop a better marriage. Be honest with your feelings, but focus on how *you* can change by applying the practice described to yourself, not your spouse.

1. How would you describe the way you currently resolve conflict in your marriage? And how would you describe the results?

2. What unresolved issue, disagreement, or recurring conflict would you most like to resolve in your marriage?

3. Would you be willing to abide by the fair-fight rules? How do you think they would work for you? How would they work for your spouse?

4. When will you call for your first fair fight? What should be the penalty for someone who violates a rule?

Once you've shared your answers, discuss what each of you needs to do as a result of your conversation.

DISCUSSION FOR A SMALL GROUP

1. What was your favorite competitive activity to watch or participate in when you were growing up? Why?

2. Are you a fan of boxing, MMA, or martial arts? Explain.

3. How did people fight in your family growing up? What practices have you adopted or deliberately tried to avoid?

4. Are you typically a good sport, a bad sport, or a no sport (someone who declines to play at all)? Why? Would your spouse agree with your self-assessment?

5. When you experience conflict, are you more likely to fight, dig your heels in, or flee? What about your spouse? How do your styles interact?

6. What do you expect to be most challenging about the process of picking a fair fight and following the fair-fight rules? Why?

7. How do you think your marriage and family would change if you learned to fight fair and resolve conflict?

8. Are you willing to commit to picking a fair fight, scheduling it, and completing at least rounds 1 through 4 before the next group meeting?

PRACTICE 4

Take a Knee or Two

A few years ago, a hundred people gathered together to attend the funeral of Trudy, a mutual friend and longtime 12Stoner (that's what we who attend 12Stone call ourselves). Trudy had been a widow for five years, and it was clear she had missed her husband, Harry, during those years. Now she had joined him in the afterlife.

After the service, Marcia and I were chatting and telling stories with a group that included Tony and Kellie, a couple we've known for more than thirty years.

"I heard they saved Harry's ashes and are planning to mix Trudy's ashes with his. That's very romantic," Kellie said with a sigh. Then with a twinkle in her eye she added, "If they ever did that with Tony and me, the ashes would involuntarily separate—or spontaneously combust!" We all fell out laughing.

To truly understand her comment, you need to know their story.

Immovable Object—Meet Irresistible Force

When I met Tony, he was dating Kellie. She was a sharp business-person and tough as nails, especially when it came to closing a deal. She was definitely what one would call a type A personality.

Tony was also in business, building a strong career in commercial real estate. He did his undergrad at Georgia Tech and then an MBA at Columbia University. He's highly accomplished, but more relaxed than Kellie. His personality is more type B.

As their pastor, I was asked to officiate their wedding. Through all their premarital counseling, they displayed the compatibility of oil and water. I playfully told them, "You two should not get married." To this day, they are the only couple I married that I ever said that to. Was I serious? Not completely. But I did foresee a lifetime of cat-and-dog encounters. They got married anyway, and it's a testament to them that they've been married for more than thirty years and have four grown kids to show for it. But they've had their battles. We've asked Tony to share just one story—our favorite—for this book. It will tell you everything you need to know about them.

A few weeks after our wedding, Kellie announced that an upcoming Friday evening would be an event called a Night of Cleaning. Being only weeks removed from being a bachelor, I couldn't imagine why *anyone* would purposely take a perfectly good Friday night and turn it into something so dreadful. However, my bride was insistent that our palatial 850-square-foot apartment receive a thorough cleaning. I wondered, *How could that take up an entire evening? And why would you want to celebrate the end of the workweek and beginning of a weekend that way?*

Among other tasks, I was assigned the responsibility of vacuuming. Shortly after the Night of Cleaning began, I got a call from my childhood best friend. Welcoming a distraction from Kellie's Friday-night party, I sat on the floor near the kitchen phone (this was before cell phones) and engaged in a lengthy conversation, laughing loudly at my buddy's account of a recent guys' trip he went on.

All of this conversation, laughter, and lounging was greatly disturbing to Kellie, so she began to clean everything around me, intentionally moving me around to let me know my time off the clock wasn't going to be tolerated. At one point, when I didn't take the hint, she began spraying some toxic cleaner on the kitchen counter, and purposely missed the surface to spray my head and face below.

This only intensified the standoff that was brewing. By the time I finished the call, it was late, and I was in no mood to vacuum. So I announced I was going to bed.

In response, Kellie took it upon herself to do my job of vacuuming, extending as much grace as she had with the kitchen counter. Well, I wasn't going to let that go. So I unplugged the vacuum.

This led to an incident-free (but highly entertaining) mock wrestling match, struggling for control of the vacuum. I was not going to concede defeat or bow to her demands. Equally stubborn, she refused to let it go. When she finally got to the wall to plug the vacuum back in, I grabbed the vacuum cleaner and held on to it for dear life.

So how did the battle end? I went to bed with the vacuum parked next to my side of the bed, the long cord wrapped around the bedpost with the end double wrapped around my right hand to secure it, just in case she tried to retrieve the vacuum while I was asleep. And yep, I did wake up with the cord tied to my hand!

The first time Marcia and I heard this story in our small group, we were dying laughing. And here's what's most remarkable: Tony and Kellie love each other and have been married a long time, but neither one of them has lost their fire.

Who's the Boss?

Maybe you and your spouse have stories like that where you're fighting for control—though yours may not be as entertaining at Tony and Kellie's. Most marriages experience power struggles to establish who's the boss and who will bow to the other's will.

> Most marriages experience power struggles to establish who's the boss and who will bow to the other's will.

When we're growing up, we know who's the boss. We start life with parents, and they are in charge. When they love you and follow God's design for your development, it's great. Parents who lead well and create a loving, healthy environment usually have kids who flourish. But even in cases where parents don't do a great job—or when we disagree with good parents—we still know they are in charge. Mom or Dad is the boss.

Then, when we go to school, our teachers and the principal are the bosses. They give us assignments to complete, rules to follow. Like it or not, they are in charge. When we learn to drive, we realize quickly the police officer is the boss when it comes to speed limits. Marcia and I have enough tickets to confirm this! And on it goes.

When you get a real job after high school or college, you have a boss. You know who the boss is, and whether or not you like that person or respect their opinions doesn't change anything. When there is disagreement, the boss makes the final decision.

Interestingly, dating relationships are different. When two people date, they engage in a relationship of equals who choose to enjoy each other. Each person retains their own individual freedom to make personal decisions. No one is the boss. Or maybe it's more accurate to say that during your dating life you remain your own boss.

But when you get married, that changes.

Oneness

Marriage is unlike any other relationship on earth. It is the *only* relationship that God ordained for oneness. God made this clear from the beginning. In the book of Genesis, soon after creation, he said, "That is why a man leaves his father and mother and is united to his wife, and they become one flesh" (2:24). And this was reaffirmed by Jesus in the New Testament:

> "Haven't you read," he replied, "that at the beginning the Creator 'made them male and female,' and said, 'For this reason a man

will leave his father and mother and be united to his wife, and the two will become one flesh'? So they are no longer two, but one flesh. Therefore what God has joined together, let no one separate." (Matt. 19:4–6)

This oneness is not a romantic notion; it is a new condition a couple enters when they get married. It's not an emotion or a feeling; it's a fact that defines who they are. And it becomes physical through sex. No wonder Jesus said that adultery is a violation of the oneness of marriage. Oneness is sacred. It is a deep bond between a man and a woman both emotionally and physically and is meant to endure until death separates them.

Here's a way to think about this idea of oneness. Marcia and I both like to drink water blended with Zipfizz. Are you familiar with this? On its website, the product is described as "a healthy and great tasting energy drink-mix powder that delivers a powerful charge of micronutrients to the body's fuel system." I simply call it a hit of vitamin B12 that gives me energy for the afternoon without the sugar crash later on. Marcia likes the fruit punch flavor, while I prefer grape. It's simple to prepare. Take a bottle of water, sip a bit off the top, pour in the Zipfizz, and give it a shake. What's my point? Once the water and Zipfizz powder are shaken together, you cannot separate them. They have become one drink. That's what marriage does to us: makes us one.

> Oneness is not a romantic notion; it is a new condition a couple enters when they get married.

Oneness is the highest value in marriage. It's much greater than *unity*. Don't get me wrong. I value unity. But if unity is like silver, then oneness is like gold. To give you a sense of the difference, as we write this, silver is selling for $17.82 per ounce while gold is trading at $1,575.40 per ounce. That makes gold eighty-eight times more valuable than silver. That's how much more valuable oneness is. When you live it out, you're experiencing marriage the way God envisioned it. You're making your marriage happier than your honeymoon, because you're experiencing *sustained* oneness as a couple, not the fleeting thrill and novelty of oneness that you felt on your honeymoon.

When a Fair Fight Ends in a Draw

Marcia and I have striven to attain and maintain this sense of oneness. That's one of the reasons we developed the fair-fight rules. We wanted to remove barriers, resolve problems, and have both our hands raised in victory together. But in our eleventh year of marriage, we had a conflict we couldn't resolve. We hit a wall. At the time, we had two kids and a six-year-old church that was finally moving from struggling to working. Then we had this conversation:

MARCIA: We have two amazing and healthy kids. I never could have imagined how enjoyable and fulfilling it would be to be a mother. Kevin, I want to have at least one more child. And we will see after that—

KEVIN: We have two amazing and healthy kids. But I

cannot come to peace with having another child. Since God has not *told* me to have a third, I cannot do it!

So what did we do? We called for a fair fight, of course. We set our time and place and did the first four rounds. And we did them again. And again. We kept working to understand the other person until we could communicate their perspective with crystal clarity and authentic empathy. And with each round, we learned more about each other. Here's how we would summarize our perspectives:

MARCIA: I grew up in a larger family, five of us kids, which my mom had within six years! My dream had always been to have *six* kids. As you might expect, when we had the first two children seventeen months apart, I was hit pretty hard by the reality of diapers, sleepless nights, and no breaks from parenting. So I downsized my dream a bit. I was pretty sure I no longer wanted six. How in the world did my mother handle five? But I knew I wanted more than two.

I love babies and the sweet bond between mother and child. And I felt I was pretty good at being a mom. If we had one more, then we would have three. That's a big shift from having six! I was *attempting* to compromise. Isn't that what the fair-fight rules were all about?

The third-child dilemma was a desire that was hard to describe. It was a deep longing in my soul that I believed God put there. I felt *called* to have more children.

KEVIN: I always thought I'd like to have a big family of six: two parents with four kids. We had Joshua first. Then seventeen months later, our girl Julisa was born. By then, my fantasy of how awesome it would be to have a big family was replaced with the reality of parenting. I loved nearly every aspect of my life, but when you put them all together, they were exhausting. I had a demanding life.

We had toughed out near financial bankruptcy to plant our church, and finally, after six years, we were just barely getting our heads above water. We had at last worked out a personal budget that might work. I was barely making enough income to cover our expenses. And at age thirty-two, I was just getting a handle on leading the church.

And now Marcia wanted to add another child? Honestly, every time I thought about it, I would have near panic attacks. I did not have the emotional margin as an individual, and we did not have the financial margin as a family. And worse, she would want a bigger house and eventually a minivan, and I would drown in silent anger and frustration.

Moving into rounds 5 through 8 was more complicated. The theme of our marriage at that time could be taken from the 1977 Dave Mason song "We Just Disagree." We couldn't get together. Neither of us was wrong, yet we still needed to find a way to compromise.

KEVIN: I told Marcia, "I cannot compromise. I feel like you're asking me to hold my breath underwater for fifteen minutes. I honestly feel like you're trying to kill me. I can't compromise."

MARCIA: I told him, "I don't know how to go forward unless you compromise. Wanting a third child is so deep within me. I'll be lost on the inside without another child because I believe this so deeply."

As a result of our impasse, our marriage was wilting like a flower without water or sunshine. We recognized that any compromise we could come up with would leave one of us feeling a deep sense of loss. We could not see a scenario where we could both win. So we went several more rounds in the fair-fight process seeking to understand each other, but we always reached a stalemate when we moved to the compromise phase. We processed, prayed, and talked, but then we would have to leave the subject alone for a few months so we could breathe. And then we did it all again.

No matter how many times we did this, we were no closer to a compromise. How could we? You can't have 25 percent or 50 percent of a child. You either have another child or you don't. There is no middle ground.

Since we were getting nowhere, we went to rounds 9 and 10. Marcia talked to some friends who understood her motherly instincts. They knew she walked with God and trusted her sense that wanting a third child was more than a whim on her part. They understood her belief that God had put this desire within her. While Marcia didn't claim having another child would be an act of obedience to God, they understood her desire was deeply spiritual.

Meanwhile, I talked with friends who understood and related to the financial pressure I was feeling. Like me, there were times when they thought this whole family thing was a better idea in concept than how it played out in real life. My feelings were further complicated by having come from a broken home and being estranged from my dad. I desperately wanted to be a good dad, to provide well, to create an emotionally healthy home, and to build a spiritually solid foundation for my family. I just could not see how that would be possible if we had another child.

During one of these conversations, a friend scoffed, "Seems to me that you're gonna lose this one. Just accept you'll be a dad of three and move on. She's got God on her side." Outwardly, I laughed with him, but on the inside I was ticked.

As much as Marcia's and my friends cared, and as much wisdom as they possessed, they were not able to help us find a resolution. We were still at a stalemate. There was only one more thing left to do: rounds 11 and 12 of the fair-fight rules. We went to a counselor.

Now, I have to be honest, I don't love going to counselors. I'm not a licensed professional counselor, but I've taken enough classes, studied enough psychology, and sat with enough people as their pastoral counselor to know how the process works. So when we discussed our dilemma with the counselor, and he started pushing and prodding and asking more questions, I got increasingly annoyed. And then he said, "Well, Kevin, I think you are just afraid. You're afraid you will end up failing to provide like your dad failed you, and this is more than you can process."

That's when I blew my top. I cussed at him and instructed him to reconsider his boundaries as a counselor. Let's just say it was not one of my best moments. On the positive side, Marcia and I traveled into new territory because he had unearthed more that was buried in her and more that was buried in me. Sadly, it only solidified our different positions.

So, for the first time in eleven years of marriage, and truthfully the only time up through today in thirty-seven years of marriage, we could not come to a mutual compromise.

> **KEVIN:** I was tired of praying and tired of talking. I was not mad at Marcia. I was sad for both of us.
>
> **MARCIA:** I told Kevin, "I know what's happening here. We keep acting like we are working through this, but really, the weeks have turned into months and the months have turned into years, and this is going to be answered by default."

She wasn't wrong. We were stuck, and neither of us knew what to do. It felt like it was eroding everything we'd fought for and won in our relationship. It was so unsettling.

Resolution for Our Impasse

Marcia and I were stuck in this same place for three years. Neither of us was proud or mean or unpleasant. But being stuck just ground away at us. Then something shifted the tectonic plates of our marriage.

MARCIA: After three years of this stalemate, I vividly remember coming to a decision. We were driving back from Michigan after visiting our families there. My yearning for a third child was as strong as ever. But we were no closer to a solution than we had been three years before. As I was sitting there in the passenger seat of the car, I finally bowed. "God," I prayed silently, "you have made it clear in Ephesians 5 that I am to submit, to honor my husband as I do you. Out of my obedience to you, I will submit to Kevin's wishes."

I told Kevin as we drove home, "You are the head of this household. If you don't want any more kids, we won't have any more. It's not what I want, but I'm tired of fighting about it. It's still going to take a long time for me to get over it. I fully expect I will have to go to counseling. That's how deep my desire is. But I will no longer fight you. Our marriage, family, and ministry are too important to let this derail them."

I said those words and, more important, I *meant* them. I didn't say them expecting to eventually get my way or to make Kevin feel guilty. I simply gave the problem to God and trusted him to take care of whatever the fallout would be.

KEVIN: I cannot express how blown away I was with my wife. I was so relieved I wanted to celebrate. She had just solved a three-year stalemate by demonstrating tremendous courage and trust in God.

Yes, I was sad for her, but I knew this was the

best decision for *us*. I thanked God that she was such a woman of faith that she was able to put in practice God's design of marriage. She had willingly trusted God by living out Ephesians 5. She chose to yield her will and submit to God through me. I was humbled by her humble spirit.

After our conversation, all I could think was, *Thank you, Jesus, for such an amazing wife.* I was glad I was finally done talking with God about this.

But he was not done talking with me!

Sometime later—I don't know how many days—I was in my prayer time, and I sensed in my spirit that God was saying to me, *So, Kevin, my son, Marcia did her part. Let's go back and read Ephesians 5 and look at your part.* So I reread it. Here's what Ephesians 5:21–31 says:

Submit to one another out of reverence for Christ.

Wives, submit yourselves to your own husbands as you do to the Lord. For the husband is the head of the wife as Christ is the head of the church, his body, of which he is the Savior. Now as the church submits to Christ, so also wives should submit to their husbands in everything.

Husbands, love your wives, just as Christ loved the church and gave himself up for her to make her holy, cleansing her by the washing with water through the word, and to present her to himself as a radiant church, without stain or wrinkle or any other blemish, but holy and blameless. In this same way, husbands ought to love their wives as their own bodies. He who loves his wife loves himself. After all, no one ever hated their own body, but they feed and care for their body, just as Christ does the church—for we are members of his body. "For this reason a man will leave his father and mother and be united to his wife, and the two will become one flesh."

It was as if God sat next to me and opened my eyes to the passage for the first time. I understood words that previously I had only read. It was clear. Of the two commands, submission is the easier one. It's like taking a knee in deference to the other person. Marcia had passed her test. *It's your turn, son*, I felt God saying to me. *Your love for her means you are to make sacrifices. Get down on both knees and serve her. You are about to have a third child.*

I almost swore again.

Have you ever wanted to put your fingers in your ears and say "La-la-la-la-la-la-la" to drown out what the other person was saying? That was this moment for me. I knew the Lord was asking me to trust his Word in Ephesians 5, to trust him anew as my family's provider, to love my wife the way Christ loved the church.

To make a long story short (okay, I know it's too late for that), I went to Marcia, I explained what God had said to me, and I offered to reverse our decision. Of course, she took me up on it and got pregnant right away. Nine months later, we welcomed child number three, Jake, into our family. And if that wasn't enough, nine *years* later, God put an exclamation point on submission for both of us by giving us a surprise: Jadon, child number four. So there you have it. We ended up with a big family of six.

Resolution for Our Marriage

Something even more important happened through this experience. We learned the fourth practice that made our marriage happier than our honeymoon. We learned mutual voluntary submission. That's where you take a knee or two in submission to each other out of love. If the word *submission* bothers you, if it seems too negative, then you can use the more positive word expressing this teaching that's found in Romans 12:10: "*Honor* one another above yourselves" (emphasis added). This is huge for a marriage. Picking fair fights brings the unity in marriage that can come from compromise, but only mutual voluntary submission can create the unmatched happiness of oneness that every married couple desires. Honoring each other above ourselves is an internal and external expression of true love.

The whole idea of submitting to each other and honoring each other out of reverence for Christ is revolutionary in a world full of people who are trying to get others to submit to them so they can impose their will on others. The thought of submitting probably seems ridiculous to a lot of people. *Why would I submit to anyone else?* they think. Or worse, they ignore it altogether and try to use Scripture to get the upper hand with their spouse. That was the case years ago when I received a random phone call from a man I didn't even know. He asked me to direct him to the Bible verse that said his wife was supposed to do what he said. I kid you not! Of course, I told him there was no verse in the Bible that said that. Instead I told him about the verse that said his role was to make sacrifices for his wife, just as Jesus did for us. That call didn't end well.

The idea behind mutual voluntary submission is about more

than humbly yielding to another person. It is an expression of living in reverence to Jesus. When you revere Christ first and foremost, you follow his guidelines for making your marriage work. *Mutual voluntary submission* is merely the term Marcia and I use to describe what Paul explained in Ephesians 5. Here's how it breaks down. First, it's *mutual*, which means we are both making this choice. Any couple who engages in mutual voluntary submission must value it and choose it or it won't work. Second, it's *voluntary*, which means it has not been forced on either of us by the other. In marriages that practice it, both parties must freely accept it. The final component, *submission*, means carrying a humble, honoring disposition. That means being able to accept a decision or direction and support it wholeheartedly, even when it may not be our preference. In other words, couples who practice mutual voluntary submission must voluntarily take a knee or two to freely bow to God's greater will for both of them. That takes incredible strength of character and requires a superior act of love.

Few things in life are more powerful than a voluntary sacrifice. It's an expression of real love that towers over our culture's silly definitions of love. Our culture exhibits a self-serving love rooted in childish wants, indulgent pleasures, dysfunctional codependence, or sullen willfulness. Real love makes sacrifices for the other person. Jesus stated it in John 15:12–13: "My commandment is this: love one another, just as I love you. The greatest love you can have for your friends is to give your life for them" (GNT). And then he demonstrated that love for us on the cross.

After Marcia and I went through the whole third-child crisis, resolved it, and learned mutual voluntary submission, we began to think of our relationship in a different way. We pictured it as a triangle with God at the top and Marcia and me at the bottom two corners.

Our desire, our goal, and our responsibility are to submit to God first in everything. As I do these things, I draw nearer to God. As a result, I move up on my side of the triangle. As Marcia does the same, she moves up on her side of the triangle. And as we both grow closer to God, we also grow closer to each other. We believe God gave us this simple yet profound insight.

GOD

We discovered in our marriage that if we made God our first love and embraced a mindset of submission to God and to each other, we could close the gap between all three of us. Submission became our outward sign of inward humility. We found it possible to die to ourselves and forgo our need to be right in reverence to Christ. Doing this changed our marriage.

Not only that, it changed our other relationships. Mutual voluntary submission became the leadership principle for the staff of 12Stone. It defined leadership. It's not about position or power; it's about honoring others above ourselves. The board of 12Stone and I practice it with each other. I submit to them, because I'm accountable to them. They submit to me because I'm their pastor and spiritual leader. This is what Jesus asks us to do as members of the church, as the body of Christ.

So let's circle back around to the question we asked earlier. Who's the boss in marriage? *God!* God is the boss of your marriage. And the two of you? You're called to oneness, not to bicker over who's the boss. Go spend some time thinking about that. If you practice taking a knee or two, it will transform your marriage. If there is the least bit of tension over who's in charge, if there is a battle of the wills, if there is confrontation about who should have the last word, you need to recognize that for what it is: you're fighting to be the boss of your marriage instead of recognizing that you already have a boss—and it's neither of you.

Mutual voluntary submission is one of the most biblically radical insights we've ever learned. It is the golden nugget at the core of oneness in a marriage. It took us years to stumble onto it, and once we discovered and practiced it as a normal part of our marriage, it transformed us. When we dated, we were two people. Once we exchanged our wedding vows and experienced our honeymoon night, we became one. But it wasn't until we practiced mutual voluntary submission and acknowledged that God was the boss of our marriage that we truly experienced the oneness we desired.

Speed Up and Slow Down

If you're looking for a practical "nonspiritual" application for how mutual voluntary submission works (we put that word in quotes because *everything* in marriage is really quite spiritual), we'll give you an example. You know Marcia is a runner and I'm not. I'm happy to go on walks with her, and we've covered many miles at that pace. However, Marcia spends many hours running every week, and I want to be with her more. So guess what I decided to do? Spend some time running with her. My goal was to be capable of running the first three miles with her. That makes me what? Her warm-up band? Anyway, after three miles, she could continue the seven, ten, fifteen, or however many miles she planned to do.

So, on many days, we run together. But we immediately discovered something the first time we did this. She's a runner and I'm at best a jogger. We don't run at the same pace. I had to speed up to be with her, and even then, she had to slow down to be with me. She has *chosen* to do that for her first three miles.

> Mutual voluntary submission means subjugating your will for the benefit of your spouse and for the oneness in your marriage.

Perhaps you're getting the picture. Marriage thrives when we figure out what it means to be in sync with each other. It usually means one person has to speed up a bit and the other has to slow down a bit. This is a principle you can apply to any area of your marriage: money management, career aspirations, the processing of emotional baggage, spiritual growth, decision making, and so on. Mutual voluntary submission means subjugating your will for the benefit of your spouse and for the oneness in your marriage.

One Knee or Two?

Over the years we've taught the concept of mutual voluntary submission to other couples and to staff. Recently we wanted to teach it to the entire congregation, so we asked our friends Jeff and Heather Semple, who are on staff at 12Stone, to demonstrate it. We picked them because they are both strong-willed and have a history of difficult challenges in their past. They have survived struggles and overcome pitfalls that many couples have had to navigate in their marriages, and they have been courageous in public sharing both their ugly seasons and their growth.

Before we tell you what the three of us demonstrated onstage, here's Jeff and Heather's story from Jeff's point of view:

Heather and I were married in Overland Park, Kansas, in the spring of 2000, surrounded by six hundred of our friends and family. The baggage each one of us brought into the relationship would just about fit inside the cargo hold of a Boeing 747, but we were sure that all the problems we had experienced before the wedding would disappear once we said our I dos. However, that plane came crashing down with us in it.

Within our first five years of marriage, I had to resign my position as a pastor from two churches because of my struggle with addiction to pornography and an inappropriate relationship with another woman. Those years were extremely painful and filled with the kinds of things we never dreamed would be part of our future. We were both dysfunctional, and that put our commitment to one another to the test.

Divorce seemed like the most obvious path forward, so we sat down to start planning how we could end our marriage. But when we looked at our daughter, who was a toddler at the time, we decided we should stay together for her. We tried talking honestly with close friends and family about our struggles, and we also met with a counselor. We did that for two years, sometimes multiple times a week, with us driving there separately most of the time.

The Holy Spirit began to do a work in both of us that mended our souls. We came to a place where we believed that staying together was not only the best for our daughter, but it was our best way to find true restoration and redemption.

After six years of fighting against and then for each other, we had our second daughter. Heather also answered a call to ministry and started seminary. At the same time, we began learning to put each other first more. Maybe our roles were not so much about who does the laundry or puts the kids to bed. Maybe our roles were better found in serving one another.

In 2007, we heard from the Lord in prayer. He told us to work together in the church. This idea was overwhelming to both of us. Could God really use two individuals who have caused so much pain and grief to people, each other, and God? In obedience, we accepted jobs at a church in northern Wisconsin. Over eleven years of ministry at that church, Heather and I experienced the favor of God in miraculous ways. And Heather became my boss for several years. Imagine how fun that was for the two of us!

I asked Jeff and Heather to come up on stage with me. They knew I was going to teach on Ephesians and what it says about marriage, but they didn't know exactly what I was going to ask them to do. A lot of people don't want to tackle that Scripture passage because of the tension over women's rights and the roles of men and women in our culture. On top of that are the theological debates over egalitarian versus complementarian points of view (we don't have time to get into all that). So all Jeff and Heather really knew was that their participation was going to be an illustration of the concept of mutual voluntary submission. And they could see that I had two props on the stage. One was a cross, representing submission to God, and the other was a tree, symbolic of the willful disobedience humanity displayed when Adam and Eve ate fruit from the tree of the knowledge of good and evil in the garden of Eden.

As we stood onstage together, I asked them a few questions and gave them the chance to talk a bit about their relationship. One of the questions I asked was whether they had chosen to follow Jesus and come to the cross in their lives, which they affirmed. (They'd better. They're both pastors on staff!) Then I read Ephesians 5:22–24:

Wives, submit yourselves to your own husbands as you do to the Lord. For the husband is the head of the wife as Christ is the head of the church, his body, of which he is the Savior. Now as the church submits to Christ, so also wives should submit to their husbands in everything.

And then I said, "These are God's directions for us in marriage. So, Heather, take a knee."

Now, Heather is a strong-willed woman and a leader by temperament and gifting. And as you know, she has been through a lot with Jeff. I had basically asked her to bow before her husband, with him standing over her. So she hesitated. But she slowly—reluctantly—got down on one knee. Not surprisingly, she didn't look excited about it.

To most people, this vulnerable position of being down on a knee feels very humbling. And in the past the church has sometimes taught only this first part of the passage without teaching the whole thing, and it has messed us up. It has created a false picture of marriage, with the husband standing tall as the head of the household, while the wife submits by taking a knee. But that misses the biblical description of the husband. So I read the following verse from Ephesians 5:25:

> Husbands, love your wives, just as Christ loved the church and gave himself up for her.

I turned to Jeff and said, "Jeff, your role as the husband is to sacrifice for your wife out of love. So get down on two knees." Jeff smiled and did what I asked, which made Heather smile. "Now both of you, stay where you are," I said, "but turn and face the cross."

I turned and addressed the congregation: "This is the true and complete picture of a biblical marriage. If submission means taking a knee, then sacrifice means taking two knees. Yes, the wife should take a knee in mutual voluntary submission to her husband, but the husband must take two knees as an act of sacrifice for his wife. But neither one is bowing to the other. Rather, they are both bowing to Christ, who gave his life on the cross for their sake."

A week after I taught this, we received a note from a husband who was a marine. He explained that he was used to taking a knee growing up playing sports and in the marines. But not two knees. He understood the significance of getting on both knees. It meant surrender—and marines never surrender. But now he was making a choice. For the sake of his marriage and to honor his wife, he was getting down on both knees in surrender to God to serve his wife.

> If submission means taking a knee, then sacrifice means taking two knees.

So what will you do? I know when I figured this out, I no longer wanted the title of head of household. I understood it meant humbling myself. It meant sacrificing for my wife. That sounded negative. But when I actually did it, and Marcia and I both engaged in mutual voluntary submission, it didn't feel demeaning. It felt freeing.

Somebody has to be willing to go first by taking a knee or two. Will it be you? Will you trust God? Are you willing to get on your knees while living in a world full of people standing up for their own rights? If you do, you will find the real gold in your marriage. You will begin to experience oneness on a level you may not have thought possible. And that's where a lot of the happiness comes from in the Second Happy.

CONVERSATION FOR A COUPLE

Answer these questions on your own, with your spouse doing the same. Then make an appointment with each other to discuss your answers. Have an honest conversation with the goal of serving each other in order to develop a better marriage. Be honest with your feelings, but focus on how *you* can change by applying the practice to yourself, not your spouse.

1. What do you find most difficult about the idea of mutual voluntary submission?

2. If you were to put yourself in the vulnerable position of submitting to your spouse, would you trust them to do the same? If not, why not?

3. Where in your marriage have you struggled the most when trying to determine who's the boss? Describe the issue as you see it.

4. Have you tried using the fair-fight rules to resolve the issue? If not, try them. If you have, and the issue is still unresolved, what specific action could you take to practice mutual voluntary submission?

Once you've shared your answers, discuss what each of you needs to do as a result of your conversation.

DISCUSSION FOR A SMALL GROUP

1. Who is the best boss you've ever had? Describe them and tell a story that illustrates why you believe this.

2. Do you have a funny story about a battle of wills in your marriage similar to the one Tony told about him and Kellie? If so, share it.

3. What happens in a relationship when there is a struggle over who's the boss?

4. What was your reaction when you read about the concept of mutual voluntary submission? How do you think practicing it would benefit a marriage, a workplace, and a community?

5. What potential challenges do you foresee in making mutual voluntary submission work in any relationship?

6. What makes it difficult for you personally to take a knee or two for your spouse?

7. In what ways have you struggled with deferring to your spouse and submitting to them as an act of love in Christlikeness?

8. How would your marriage change if you practiced mutual voluntary submission? Are you willing to commit to trying mutual voluntary submission in your marriage? When and how will you do so?

PRACTICE 5

Don't Settle for the Hollow Easter Bunny

Have you ever been in a situation where everything seemed to fall apart? Where it went from bad to worse? One of our favorite stories illustrating this was told to us by Dan and Patti Reiland, wonderful friends and ministry partners for more than nineteen years. It occurred to them many years ago, before they had kids, when they were living in San Diego.

Their friends, Bill and Diane Samson, asked them to house-sit for fourteen days while they were on vacation. Dan and Patti were happy to do it. After all, the Samsons were an older couple who were doing well and had a large, beautiful home with a pool. Dan and Patti would still be working during the day, but at night it would be like a vacation. However, in this case, *house-sitting* really meant *zoo-keeping*, because the house was full of animals, starting with a huge Saint Bernard who had lived far beyond her expected life span. She was blind, deaf, and clueless. Barely able to get around, she drooled uncontrollably. Add to her one bird, three lop-eared rabbits, four lunatic cats, five exotic tropical fish, and five koi. Just in case you're not familiar with koi, they're large specialty fish, like big goldfish, only a lot more expensive. Bill loved his and had names for each of them.

The last thing Bill and Diane said to Dan before they left was "Our Saint Bernard is old. Really old. She's supposed to be dead already, according to the vet. So she will probably die on your watch." That must have been unnerving. "Don't sweat it if she does," they continued. "We sorta wish she would. It would be easier on us and better for her. So if you wake up and she's not breathing, it's okay!"

According to Dan:

Bill and Diane's house was on the edge of the desert next to a canyon. We were there only one night when tragedy struck. The coyotes traveled up through the canyon in the night, came around the beautiful pool, and went to the front of the house, where the rabbit cages were located. They destroyed every one of the Samsons' prized lop-eared rabbits. It was not a pretty sight. Blood and guts were all over the driveway, and bunny fur was everywhere.

We were horrified, so we called their son-in-law. But when he came over, he thought it was more hilarious than horrible. He decided to put yellow police tape around the driveway where all the dead rabbits were, like it was a crime scene. Then he used chalk to outline the bodies, took photographs, and started interrogating me!

I felt like I'd failed my friends and wanted the mess gone, while he was trying to turn it into a joke.

Now, I don't know what happened to the air-conditioning unit. Patti and I like it cold. But apparently the very special parrot didn't. There it was on day two, lying on the bottom of the cage, stone dead. Patti and I were stunned.

We never actually witnessed the demise of the four cats. All we can assume is that the coyotes came back for them. We say that because these four cats, who *never* missed a meal, simply didn't show up for their food one day. And no one has seen them since.

I was really getting nervous when one of the koi died around day nine. House-sitting was turning into the killing fields, and I knew I had to do something. Only I didn't know what to do. One dead koi turned into two, and I still had no idea why. All I knew was that I was feeling *really* bad.

I thought, *I know what to do. The koi need more oxygen. Sure, they've been living in that pond for years just fine, but oxygen will do the trick*. Okay, I was panicking, but I had to do something!

So in one brilliant move, I took the air pump from the aquarium, where the beautiful and rare tropical fish lived, and set it up outside by the koi pond. *I'll borrow it for just a little while, not long*, I thought.

I put the pump's hose into the pond and watched bubbles of life-giving oxygen rise up in the water, thinking it would be my salvation. But it wasn't. Two more of the koi died. That meant there was only one of Bill's precious babies left: Harvey.

I was determined to save the last one! Bill would feel better, or at least less angry, if there was one koi left. "God being my helper, Harvey is going to be the survivor," I declared.

My last thought was, *There must be something bad in the water.* So to save Harvey, I took him out of the pond and put him in a large bucket of fresh water before I left for work.

When I got home, I discovered that Harvey, the last koi, had done a double gainer out of the bucket. There he lay, next to the pool, hard as a rock.

I felt terrible. I had allowed five koi, four cats, three rabbits, and one rare parrot to die. In my distress, I had forgotten to put the pump back in the aquarium. After a couple of days, all the tropical fish died.

When Bill and Diane got home, they found Patti crying and me struggling to break the news to them. When I did, they were stunned. They didn't know what to think when they realized the only creature from their family zoo who was still alive was their ancient Saint Bernard!

Believe it or not, Dan and Patti's friendship with Bill and Diane survived their house-sitting experience. And now Dan enjoys telling that story anytime he wants to talk about dealing with adversity when everything goes wrong.

It's easy to laugh when we hear a story like Dan's, but it's not so funny if the story is about a couple's marriage falling apart. Marcia and I have heard more than our share of these stories over the years. Dan's "killing fields" story was one of ignorance, bad luck, and bad choices under pressure. It was a perfect storm. We hope the story of your marriage isn't one of those, but we feel certain you are under pressure in your marriage. Why? Because everyone's marriage is. What kinds of choices are you making under the pressure? How is your relationship holding up? More important, what determines how it will hold up in the future?

Which Bunny Is Which?

How do marriages survive the pressures of life? How can we know which will thrive, which will merely survive, and which will die? We've already mentioned that if you'd looked at our marriage in the first few years, you might have been convinced we were destined for divorce. But here we are, happily married after thirty-seven years. You've probably looked at another couple and thought, *They're going to make it. They'll be great together.* Yet that marriage didn't survive. What enables a marriage to hold together and thrive?

To answer this question during a weekend sermon series, I decided to illustrate it with two bunnies. No, not the kind the coyotes devoured. And not the kind that gets pulled out of a hat. There's really no magic that makes a marriage suddenly work; a happy, lasting marriage takes time and effort. No, for this example, I used chocolate Easter bunnies.

When I was a kid, I always looked forward to getting a chocolate bunny in my Easter basket, and I always hoped it would be solid. But you could never tell by just looking at it. On Easter mornings the first thing I did was pull it out of the packaging to find out. Usually, to my disappointment, the bunny I received was hollow. My parents had settled for the hollow bunny!

The difference between solid and hollow bunnies was my inspiration for an illustration that teaches a bigger truth. One Sunday I put two giant chocolate bunnies on a table onstage. They were not just any bunnies. They were the Easter bunnies of my childhood dreams: milk chocolate sculptures standing two feet tall. I had them made by special order and shipped to us. They looked identical. They were, in fact, the same height, made from the same chocolate, using the exact same mold. But as you may have already guessed, one was solid and weighed a hefty twelve pounds while the other was hollow and weighed a fourth of that.

How could I show the difference between the two? I put pressure on them. I put my hands on the first bunny and squeezed as hard as I could. Nothing happened. I couldn't move it, change it, or even put a dent in it. Then I did the same thing to the second bunny. It crumbled in my hands and fell apart faster than Dan's attempt to take care of the Samsons' menagerie.

Marriages are like those bunnies. On the outside they can look good and solid, and nobody can tell what they're made of. But put some pressure on them—and every marriage experiences pressure—and you'll find out whether they're really solid.

How marriages stand up is determined by what's inside. The hollow ones will crack and crumble under pressure. But those that have been built solidly can take it. Squeeze them all you want, and they are unmoved, unshaken, unaltered, unharmed.

A solid marriage, like a solid bunny, weighs more, costs more, and withstands more. It's got substance. It's been "filled up" on the inside with wise principles, tested practices, good decisions, and painstaking discipline. The process of making it solid isn't quick, cheap, or easy. But it's worth it, because solid marriages last under pressure.

A Solid Bunny Is Like . . .

When Jesus taught this same principle, he used a different metaphor:

> Therefore everyone who hears these words of mine and puts
> them into practice is like a wise man who built his house on the
> rock. The rain came down, the streams rose, and the winds blew
> and beat against that house; yet it did not fall, because it had its
> foundation on the rock. But everyone who hears these words of
> mine and does not put them into practice is like a foolish man
> who built his house on sand. The rain came down, the streams
> rose, and the winds blew and beat against that house, and it fell
> with a great crash. (Matt. 7:24–27)

You could substitute the word *marriage* for *house* in that passage
and it would reveal truth. The wise couple builds their marriage on
the rock of Jesus's words. And then when the storms and winds of
life beat against that marriage, it does not fall. Why? Rock is solid.
But couples who don't build their marriages on something solid will
fall with a great crash. They're like hollow bunnies.

We want to make sure you notice something about the parable
of the wise and foolish builders. The houses were the same. So were
the storms. One house didn't experience a gentle shower while the
other experienced a hurricane. In both cases, the storm is described
exactly the same: "The rain came down, the streams rose, and the
winds blew and beat against that house." The difference was the
foundation on which the two houses were built: one was on a solid
foundation; the other was on an unstable foundation.

We often want to blame what's falling apart in our lives on the strength of the storm. But in truth, everyone's life experiences storms. Everyone's marriage experiences challenges. Everyone has to deal with difficult finances. Everyone faces temptations that test their character. No one escapes intense trials and storms. Some crumble under the pressure while others stand strong because of what is on the inside.

If you grew up in a home with Christ-following parents who had a solid marriage, you probably know how this works. Their efforts and example have made an investment in you that makes you solid, so that pressure won't make you fall apart. The home Marcia grew up in, while not perfect, was solid. Mine, on the other hand, was hollow. My parents divorced when I was in middle school. Sure, we went to church and talked about God's wisdom, but we simply did not put it into practice. Knowing you need a solid foundation doesn't give you one. Neither does talking about it. You have to actually *build* it by living it.

> We often want to blame what's falling apart in our lives on the strength of the storm. But in truth, everyone's life experiences storms.

That's what Jesus was telling us in the parable. The wisdom he brings gives life. The principles and practices we learn from him help us to build something solid in our lives, including our marriages. We learn how to handle our calendars, cash, conflicts, and options.

Build It Ten Times

I had a close friend (we'll call him Steve) who knew solid principles but never consistently put them into practice. After about ten years of ups and downs without any evident progress, he was so frustrated with his life that he complained profusely to me one weekend.

Thinking about his brother, he said, "I work as hard as my brother in life, and I never get ahead. It's just not fair." I could see his level of frustration. And I understood it. He *had* worked hard in life. But he was hollow. I decided to have a very candid conversation with him. I used his children's wooden building blocks to explain. I put two short blocks on the ground, spaced apart, and placed one long one on top of them.

"This is like a one-story building," I said, "right?"

He nodded.

I knocked it down and rebuilt it. Then I did it again. I built it and knocked it down nine times, and then built it again for a tenth time and left it standing. "How many stories do I have here?" I asked.

"One," Steve replied.

Then I started all over again to create another scenario. I built one story, but instead of knocking it down, I constructed another story on top of it. Then another. I built ten stories, one on top of another, without knocking them down. "How many stories does this have?" I asked.

"Ten," Steve replied.

"In each scenario, I worked equally hard, right? I built ten stories," I said. "But because I knocked the first story down every time in the first scenario, I was never able to build anything higher than a single story. Knocking down the building every time has a high cost.

"Steve," I said, "the first scenario is your life. You save your money with great discipline for nine or more months. And then something snaps, and you take an unplanned trip or make a big unnecessary purchase, emptying your savings. Afterward, you regret it, and you start over again. You do this over and over. What takes you eleven months to build up, you knock down in one month of emotionally mismanaged decisions. And you keep doing it.

"Your brother, on the other hand, never stops practicing solid principles. He saves for twelve months of the year with high discipline. He lives within his means, meager as they are. He has developed emotional muscle. He never blew his budget on the cars or motorcycles or trips or furniture that you did. Every year, as you started over, he built on top of what he already had."

Then I carefully offered my observation: "Sure, it may have cost him 75 percent more emotional muscle and discipline. But at the end of ten years, he had ten times more than you. He paid the price to build solid, while you made hollow decisions."

I was not trying to be unkind. I was stating the unfortunate truth. This pattern in Steve's life made him feel hollow. He'd be responsible in his interactions with his wife for a while, but then his temper would blow, doing damage to their relationship. In his job, he'd be diligent for a season, but then he'd get sloppy. He'd then quit that job and chase another, starting over. This happened in his faith too. He'd attend church for several months, but then he would disappear for a while. He'd maintain a prayer life, until he would not. He was always trying to find shortcuts whenever things got hard, instead of building a solid life. That created instability in his home, because he never consistently lived according to the same set of values. When he felt pressure, he collapsed, and his world fell apart. Then he'd find himself having to rebuild from scratch again.

Steve's brother had paid a price emotionally not to blow his budget, not to lose his temper, not to abandon his faith practices. He consistently paid the cost all along, instead of indulging himself and having to pay the price on the back end.

As I tried to help Steve, Marcia and I watched him and learned a lot of lessons for ourselves. We concluded that just as it takes 75 percent more chocolate to make a bunny solid rather than hollow, it takes 75 percent more effort to build a solid marriage and family instead of a hollow one. What does that mean? It means being much more intentional about investing in your marriage and living your principles consistently day after day.

Faith Nonnegotiables

Even though our marriage wasn't very stable in the early years, fortunately our faith was. That made a huge difference. We never had any confusion about who gets center stage in the universe: Jesus. Colossians 1:15–17 says,

> The Son [Jesus] is the image of the invisible God, the firstborn
> over all creation. For in him all things were created: things in

heaven and on earth, visible and invisible, whether thrones or powers or rulers or authorities; all things have been created through him and for him. He is before all things, and in him all things hold together.

That's pretty conclusive: *all* things were created by Jesus and for him, and he holds them *all* together. Since we are convinced Jesus is the center of existence, we made him the center of our marriage and family.

Here's why this is important. If Jesus is *not* at the center, then someone else will be. That means the husband or wife or kids will be vying for center stage. So Marcia and I acknowledge that Jesus is and should be the center, and we build everything around him. It means we build on his wisdom, his solid rock. This decision sets up everything else in our life: our career, our calendar, our cash, and our character.

For that reason, from the very beginning, Marcia and I decided we would build on the stability of Christ and his teachings. That doesn't mean we did it perfectly, but we did do it intentionally. We made these values sacred in our marriage. By *sacred* we mean they are set apart from everything else in our marriage and family. They are revered, cherished, the top priority. They serve as our family code.

That's where we suggest you start as you work to bring solidity to your marriage. The nonnegotiables of faith should become the rock-solid foundation that will give you strength as a couple. Let them make you solid from the inside out. And then when the storms come, your marriage and family can stand instead of fall apart.

While we could create an endless list of nonnegotiables, that would not be helpful. So we'll focus on the three that have set the pattern for our life.

1. SPEND TIME WITH GOD DAILY

Marcia and I each spend time nearly every day in Scripture and in prayer. The Bible is one big story, the story of God's interaction with humankind. (If you want to gain insight on that story, my book *Grown-Up Faith* unpacks it.) The Bible also contains God's wisdom for life. The more you read and interact with the Bible, the better you understand God's character and principles.

> The nonnegotiables of faith should become the rock-solid foundation that will give you strength as a couple.

Prayer fosters a relationship with God that helps us build additional life-giving relationships with others, including in marriage. It provides the power of God to help us defeat our self-centeredness and gives us the grace to be focused on others. This is the point in James 4:1–10, which we looked at earlier:

> What causes fights and quarrels among you? Don't they come from your desires that battle within you? You desire but do not have, so you kill. You covet but you cannot get what you want, so you quarrel and fight. You do not have because you do not ask God. When you ask, you do not receive, because you ask with wrong motives, that you may spend what you get on your pleasures.

You adulterous people, don't you know that friendship with the world means enmity against God? Therefore, anyone who chooses to be a friend of the world becomes an enemy of God. Or do you think Scripture says without reason that he jealously longs for the spirit he has caused to dwell in us? But he gives us more grace. That is why Scripture says:

> "God opposes the proud
> but shows favor to the humble."

Submit yourselves, then, to God. Resist the devil, and he will flee from you. Come near to God and he will come near to you. Wash your hands, you sinners, and purify your hearts, you double-minded. Grieve, mourn and wail. Change your laughter to mourning and your joy to gloom. Humble yourselves before the Lord, and he will lift you up.

How do we humble ourselves before the Lord? How do we come near to God? Through prayer. I don't know about you, but if I am disconnected from God, I become a less pleasant person. My temper gets short. So does my patience. I am less likely to be kind, to give grace, or to be generous. For those reasons—and simply for the sake of being close to my heavenly Father—I do everything I can to spend time with God every day.

2. WORSHIP GOD TOGETHER WEEKLY

We live our lives daily. But most of us plan our lives weekly. God knew this when he created the Sabbath, the Lord's day, and established it from the very beginning at the creation of the world. In Exodus 20:8–11, God commanded,

> Remember the Sabbath day by keeping it holy. Six days you shall labor and do all your work, but the seventh day is a sabbath to the LORD your God. On it you shall not do any work, neither you, nor your son or daughter, nor your male or female servant, nor your animals, nor any foreigner residing in your towns. For in six days the LORD made the heavens and the earth, the sea, and all that is in them, but he rested on the seventh day. Therefore the LORD blessed the Sabbath day and made it holy.

We won't get too deep into the theology here, but God directed the Jews to keep the Saturday Sabbath by resting and worshipping him, which they did for thousands of years. And when Jesus rose from the dead and established the church, its leaders chose to honor him by changing their Sabbath to Sunday, resurrection day. For two thousand years since, the church has gathered on the Lord's day to worship him.

As a couple and as a family, we have practiced weekly worship. Because I'm a pastor, we may have to do it differently than you do. We worship together every Sunday, whether we're home or traveling or on vacation. When you're consumed with your own problems and ambitions all week, worshipping God reminds you of what's really important. It puts Jesus back at the center of our lives if we've drifted off course in our thinking. But Sunday can't be a rest day for me, obviously. So for almost as long as Marcia and I have been married, my rest day has been Thursday. We protect it fiercely because it lets us breathe.

If you work a traditional schedule, you can keep the Lord's day on Sunday as a faith nonnegotiable. If you don't, you may need to be creative, as we have. If you're working on Sundays, you may need to worship God using online resources, like the ones our church offers at 12Stone.com, or join a small group that worships together on a different day of the week. You may need to split your worship and rest days, as we do. If you can arrange as a couple to worship together and rest together, that's ideal. But work something out. It will help your relationship with God and with your spouse and family.

3. PUT GOD FIRST IN FINANCES ALWAYS

From the day we got married, Marcia and I have arranged our finances with Jesus as the center. That means we have always given the *first* 10 percent of our income, the tithe, to the church where we worship. Malachi 3:10 says,

> "Bring the whole tithe into the storehouse, that there may be food in my house. Test me in this," says the LORD Almighty, "and see if I will not throw open the floodgates of heaven and pour out so much blessing that there will not be room enough to store it."

We believe giving the tithe (meaning tenth) is the beginning of obedient giving. We do it consistently, and anytime God prompts us to give, we do so on top of our tithe.

Since Marcia and I acknowledge Jesus as the Lord and Savior at the center of our lives and marriage, we can't become economic atheists in our finances. We prayerfully set an annual budget that we believe honors Christ, and then we work together to follow it, keeping each other accountable to live within it. God is our provider, and we are the stewards of all he has given us.

In order to best honor God financially, we live by the 10/10/80 rule as our framework. We give the first 10 percent back to God in our tithe. We try to put the second 10 percent into our savings. (We first created an emergency fund. Then we put money into traditional savings or retirement, even if we are only able to swing 2 or 5 percent.) The remaining 80 percent is what we live on. That includes all expenses: taxes, housing, utilities, food, cars, vacations, clothes—everything.

We also learned that credit cards can be a prison, not a source of freedom. Proverbs 22:7 says, "The rich rule over the poor, and the borrower is slave to the lender." So we paid off our credit cards in our first five years of marriage and have never carried a credit card balance since. We use credit cards for convenience, not to borrow money for purchases.

Why are we going into this detail? Because if you want a solid marriage and a solid life, you have to put solid principles into practice. When God is first in your life in the places that matter most—your heart, your time, and your finances—everything else has a better chance of staying on track. You won't be constantly knocking down the blocks of your life and having to rebuild them over and over.

Family Nonnegotiables

If you want a solid marriage, you have to keep sacred the things God asks you to keep sacred. That way Jesus remains at the center of your life and your marriage. But you get to decide on the practices you believe are important for your family culture and your family code. These values and practices will help to make your marriage and family solid.

These nonnegotiables will not be the same for every marriage and family. You will probably choose them based on your personal history and your aspirations. Marcia and I will tell you about the four things we decided made the most sense for our lives together. We hope they will help you to identify yours.

1. TOGETHERNESS

Marcia and I decided to build our marriage around the idea of togetherness. What we noticed early on was that many marriages and families have a default setting of separateness, meaning that unless they *plan* to be together, the expectation was that each did their own thing on their own. We don't have any criticism for those marriages. However, what we noticed was that most relationships naturally drift apart, not together, if couples aren't intentional about doing things together.

So we made togetherness our default practice. Now, having a night out with friends on your own or spending time alone is fine. But our regular daily expectation is that we will be home together unless we have specifically planned and agreed to do otherwise. We believe that to build a solid marriage and family, we have to be very intentional about sharing our lives and staying close.

> To build a solid marriage and family, we have to be very intentional about sharing our lives and staying close.

MARCIA: We set Thursdays aside every week for a date night together. They are sacred. We protect them from any intrusions, which can be a challenge. In the beginning, we would dine out on the dollar menu at McDonald's and then watch a movie at the sketchy local dollar theater. And when I say sketchy, I'm not kidding. The popcorn and sodas cost more than the tickets. Murders had been committed there, and I don't mean just on the screen!

It is a night I always look forward to. No kids. No interruptions. We just talk to each other about the future, about politics, about sex, about struggles, or sometimes we just chill. As we already said, we try very hard not to make it a fair-fight night. Why would we want to waste a date night on fighting?

KEVIN: We also set the calendar for a weekly family night. All the kids who still lived at home had to be present from dinner to bedtime, usually from 6:00 p.m. to 9:00 p.m. We would often let the kids choose the meal, whether homemade pizzas or Mom's amazing buffalo chicken dip or takeout from someone's favorite restaurant. Dinnertime was filled with stories about what was going on with friends, sports, and school, or we'd talk about what was going on in the world.

We used this one night a week to make family memories together. Sometimes the nights were dedicated to the kids' sporting events or band concerts, but we'd go as one family and support that person.

Marcia and I are convinced that no matter how you slice it, love is spelled t-i-m-e. Prioritizing togetherness gives us time together. Through the years, consistent family nights proved to be the mortar that helped cement us and our kids together. And date nights kept Marcia and me close. It made us solid.

2. SPEAKING THE TRUTH IN LOVE

Marcia and I grew to recognize that when it comes to the truth, ignorance is not bliss, and pretending that something isn't true doesn't make it go away. Instead it creates pretense, and that is destructive. What, then, are we to do? Ephesians 4:15 says, "Speaking the truth in love, we will grow to become in every respect the mature body of him who is the head, that is, Christ."

We made speaking the truth in love sacred. We chose to make the practice of telling each other the truth—and doing it in a way that was kind and loving—deeply important to us, so important that we describe it as its own practice in this book: evict the elephant (practice 6). We encourage you to dig into it later. But in the meantime, we'll just say this: pretense, which is ignoring the truth and hoping it will go away, is one of the most unrecognized destructive forces in marriages and families. Speaking the truth to each other in love is a powerful practice in battling that force, and the freedom it brings is amazing.

3. GUMPTION

You have probably observed that, in life, there are climbers who strive for things and there are campers who settle for things. Marcia and I choose to be climbers. We choose to take on challenges. We require ourselves to grow. We take risks. We make the effort to train our talents. And we work hard. To describe this value, we landed on the word *gumption*. What is gumption? It's a term related to self-leadership. Our family defines it as the character to commit and complete. Some might use words such as *grit*, *chutzpah*, or *determination*. Whatever you call it, it's *committing* to strive toward the summit instead of stopping to camp halfway up the mountain. It's not quitting because something gets difficult. It's paying the price to complete the climb. That's gumption, and it's a nonnegotiable value in our family.

MARCIA: I graduated from college with a music education degree, but I had always talked about getting a master's as well. I worked as a music teacher for several years until we started a family, and then chose to stay home and be a career mom. More than once when finances were tight, I had to return to teaching part-time to make ends meet. Needless to say, there was no money for a master's degree.

When our third child went to school, I began dreaming again of working on a master's, but instead we were surprised by Jadon, our fourth child! I went back into mommy mode again. As Jadon grew more self-sufficient, the way finally seemed clear for me to work on that degree.

I dove in with excitement, but soon all the fun of *dreaming* about going back to school turned into two grueling years of papers, online discussions, and endless reading. Often I felt like quitting. At those times, I relied on gumption. Instead of quitting, I dug in, and in 2015, I earned my master's from a seminary.

KEVIN: The church never would have survived in its early years if Marcia and I hadn't possessed gumption. When we planted 12Stone Church more than thirty years ago, our goal was to start as a church of two hundred because we knew it would create momentum for reaching spiritually unresolved people.

Before we launched, we talked with thousands in the community, and eight hundred committed to attend our first service. Realistically, we hoped four hundred would show up on that first weekend, with two hundred returning the second weekend.

On launch day we missed our goal by 75 percent. One hundred and four people showed up. The next week, attendance dropped to half of that. For a long time, we called ourselves the Heinz 57 Church. Why? Because we had fifty-seven people attend each weekend for many months. It was like Dan at the Samsons' house. Everything was falling apart for us.

Marcia and I lived under the pressure of leading a struggling church for five years! It was not until our sixth year that we reached the two hundred people we'd expected at the launch. What got us through those years was gumption.

MARCIA: So far, all our kids have shown gumption as well. From getting black belts in karate, to competing on the swim team, to challenging for first chair in the orches-tra, to playing sports like football, soccer, or golf. We all aspire. And as the children have grown older, they have used the emotional muscle they built in their younger years to continue to climb.

Josh showed gumption when he passed the incredibly demanding CPA exams. To become a reading recovery specialist, our daughter, Julisa, showed gumption by completing a two-year program while being a teacher full-time. And our third child, Jake, displayed it when he received his CPA certification faster than anyone in the history of the college from which he graduated. Yes, we have two CPAs in our family, but they didn't get their math skills from me! And Jadon, who's currently in high school, is walking in the footsteps of his siblings. None of us believe in sitting back and waiting for our big break. We believe in working hard in order to be ready when our opportunities come.

We believe life is too challenging *not* to make gumption one of our nonnegotiable family values. It has served us well, and maybe it will do the same for your family.

4. BLESSING OTHERS

It's the nature of God to bless us, but when he does, it's not merely so that we *feel* blessed. It's so that we can share that blessing with others. That not only helps others, but it also makes us more like our Father in heaven, who blessed us by giving his only son for us (John 3:16).

Recognizing God's giving nature compelled us to make *blessing others* one of our nonnegotiable values. To Marcia and me, that means not seeing ourselves as a reservoir of God's kindness, but as a river that passes his kindness along to others. We demonstrate that by maintaining caring hearts, serving others, and giving money to others. Sometimes it's as simple as how we treat the homeless guy named Bob in our area. Or we pay for someone's coffee at the local shop. Or we anonymously buy dinner for someone at a restaurant.

I'm happy to say this behavior has become common among the people in our church. Many evenings, multiple meals at a restaurant get covered by 12Stoners. In fact, on a recent night, when Marcia and I asked for the bill at a local restaurant, the waitress handed it to us and said, "Here it is, all paid for." At the bottom of the receipt was written, "Thanks for saving our marriage and family. A grateful 12Stoner." We were grateful that our dinner was paid for, but we were even more grateful that we'd helped another family.

Is blessing others always easy for us? Of course not. Marcia will tell you a story about a time when it was a challenge for us:

MARCIA: Our oldest son, Josh, met his first college roommate as a freshman on move-in day. While we were settling Josh in, his roommate's parents were doing the same for their son. I noticed they were having trouble getting his computer to work. It was an older model, and it wouldn't work with the college's system. After trying numerous ways to fix the problem and becoming completely exasperated, they finally gave up and told their son he would just have to use the computers in the library when he needed one for schoolwork.

The young man's mother was clearly upset. I felt her pain. Her desire to give her son the tools he needed for success at school collided with the pretty hefty cost of supplying a new computer. I really wanted to help, but we weren't in much better shape. We had been able to give Josh the computer he needed, but it had been a stretch. Still, it was a burden on my heart that I couldn't shake off after we returned home.

Then God gave me an idea. I had a ring that was quite valuable. Not my wedding ring, but an anniversary ring that was worth about the price of a computer. Kevin had given it to me several years before. It was the most expensive piece of jewelry I owned. To me it had great sentimental value because it represented the twenty-five years we had been married at that time, and how much we had grown and endured in those years.

I didn't really want to part with the ring, but I knew God was asking me to bless that mom and her son with a computer. I felt I couldn't just pray about it and hope a computer would magically appear. I had to *do* something about it. So after talking it over with Kevin, we decided to sell the ring and use the money to buy the roommate a computer.

We received a note from his mom thanking us for what we had done. But the true gift I received was the peace and joy I felt by blessing them. As a mom myself, I knew she would be more at ease knowing her son had what he needed.

Blessing others can feel like it has a cost, but you don't lose when you bless others; you actually get blessed all the more. We value it highly, and we hope you do too.

> You don't lose when you bless others; you actually get blessed all the more.

Are you prepared to do the work of building a solid marriage based on good values? From the very beginning of our marriage, Marcia and I chose to follow our faith nonnegotiables. My mom gave me a great start in my faith when I was growing up, and Marcia's parents did the same for her. That helped us to have a solid start. But we had to identify and practice the other nonnegotiables along the way, some before we had kids and others after our first was born. You will have to make your own decisions about the nonnegotiables in your marriage and family. And you'll need to follow through by living them out if you want to avoid having a hollow marriage. When you do, you will build the kind of marriage that withstands pressure.

Solid Under Pressure

In the best-case scenario, you would begin creating the solid foundation and framework of values for your marriage even before you meet the person you would marry. Once engaged, the two of you would share them and come to an agreement on your values as a couple and start living them even before your wedding day. That way, from day one of your marriage, your relationship would already be solid.

That's how I would describe the journey of Kristi, the daughter of our close friends Chris and Lisa Huff. On May 18, 2008, I officiated Kristi's wedding to Cole. I had watched her grow up. She was adorable as a child and no less beautiful as a bride. I was thrilled to perform the ceremony and tell their friends and family, "Just as Jesus Christ is the Lord of their lives, he will be the solid foundation that holds their marriage firm." I knew Kristi had a strong foundation, and I had seen how she and Cole had already begun building on it together. I was confident they would never fall for the hollow Easter bunny!

Kristi is one of those rare thirty-five-year-olds whose parents are still together. She was in first grade when her father accepted Christ, changing the trajectory of his family for his and future generations. As a result, Kristi grew up in church. At home, Chris and Lisa spent intentional time teaching and investing in Kristi and her two brothers. The Huff family embraced and practiced the same faith nonnegotiables Marcia and I did. "It was our family, our community. It was just what we did," Kristi said.

Cole had been blessed with a stepfather who taught him values he still holds dear today: be a man of your word, do your best, and work hard for the little guy. For most of Cole's life he was an only child, so he found community on the soccer field, where his coaches invested in him. Those relationships inspired Cole to work at a Christian summer camp, and that led to his accepting Christ.

Kristi and Cole met as students at Berry College near Rome, Georgia. Each walked away from their first date with different impressions. Kristi scribbled in her journal, "I'm not sure it's going to work." But Cole thought, *I could marry her!* Fortunately for Cole, Kristi was intrigued enough to continue dating him. As their relationship became more serious, they realized for a healthy union to exist they needed to have a foundation of values. They discussed their non-negotiables *before* marriage and learned they were in alignment. No sex before marriage. No living together before marriage, but spend plenty of time together, including at church. When they married, they would continue to tithe. Divorce would never be an option.

Like all couples, they faced challenges, starting in the first year they were married. It's hard for the honeymoon phase to last when you move far from home and you're poor. Cole was attending law school in Boston without financial support from his family. His hours were long, and their schedules often had them going in different directions. Kristi's desire for planning often clashed with Cole's "it will all work out" mindset. For a long time, they couldn't find a church in Boston, and Kristi greatly missed that sense of community. She entered a dark season as a result.

After three years, they got the chance to move back to Atlanta, and they were once again close to family and back at 12Stone. Soon they had their daughter Evelyn. But that only led to the next round of pressure: parenting. Even with the support of family, learning to parent is a challenge. Kristi, the planner, dove into books and mommy blogs for wisdom on baby raising and sleep schedules. But babies apparently don't read those things. When nothing seemed to work, she and Cole would fight in the middle of the night.

If this sounds familiar, it's because all marriages deal with pressures like these. Pressure from parenting, fighting, spending, household duties. Cole and Kristi learned pretty quickly that a babysitter is worth every penny. And they learned how to date as a married couple. When Cole felt led to adopt, he and Kristi argued about it. But they worked it out. Today they are a family of five. Why does it still work? Because their marriage remains based on solid principles, and they are committed to each other.

Which Bunny Do You Choose?

How your marriage weathers life's storms has little to do with the severity of the storms. What's inside you will always determine whether your marriage falls apart or stands strong. So we have to ask: How will you build your marriage? Which bunny will you choose? Are you willing to do the work to create the solid bunny? Or are you going to just hope that a hollow one holds up when the pressure comes?

If you're early in your life and marriage, or if you're currently engaged, the best thing you can do is to start filling your relationship with solid values. You don't have to believe what the culture tells you, that divorce is likely in your future. You can take a stand. Start by making Jesus the center of your relationship. Together, embrace the nonnegotiables of your faith, and make them sacred in your life so that your career, calendar, cash, and character are built on them. Then together choose your additional nonnegotiables for creating a solid, happy, lasting marriage and family.

But maybe you have already had one hollow marriage fall to pieces, gone through a divorce, and remarried. Or perhaps you're in your forties, fifties, sixties, or seventies. Know this: it's never too late to build a more solid marriage. However, we need to be forthright with you. It will be harder than if you had started in your twenties or early thirties. If you've been married for a long time, you may have already made hollow decisions and your marriage may already be cracking. Our encouragement to you is to not give up. Even if you have mistakes to overcome and damage to undo, God can and will help you.

> The best thing you can do is to start filling your relationship with solid values.

Remember that life probably will not become *less* challenging. You're not likely to have *fewer* problems tomorrow. All the pressures of life won't suddenly disappear. So think about what building a more solid marriage would do for you, your spouse, and your children or grandchildren. Use the practices as your guide. You won't regret it.

CONVERSATION FOR A COUPLE

Answer these questions on your own, with your spouse doing the same. Then make an appointment with each other to discuss your answers. Have an honest conversation with the goal of serving each other in order to develop a better marriage. Be honest with your feelings, but focus on how *you* can change by applying the practice to yourself, not your spouse.

1. How committed and successful have you been in living out the faith nonnegotiables listed in the practice? Why have you succeeded or failed with each?
   - Spend time with God daily.
   - Worship God together weekly.
   - Put God first in finances always.

2. How would you describe the differences between your and your spouse's attitudes toward these biblical principles in marriage? What might be the source of those differences?

3. What other family nonnegotiables would you like to see embraced and practiced in your marriage and family?

4. How would you personally need to change to build a more solid marriage? What would you need to start doing differently?

Once you've shared your answers, discuss what each of you needs to do as a result of your conversation.

DISCUSSION FOR A SMALL GROUP

1. Have you ever experienced anything like Dan and Patti Reiland's animal disaster where everything seemed to go wrong or fall apart? If so, share the story.

2. In your family, growing up, did you practice any faith nonnegotiables? If so, what were they, and how did they influence you?

3. In your family, growing up, were there any other nonnegotiables? If so, what were they, and how did they influence you?

4. How would you describe the bunny of your marriage? Is it more solid or more hollow? Would you describe the chocolate as sweet, bittersweet, or unsweetened? Why?

5. In the story with the building blocks, who did you relate to more: Steve or his more consistent brother? Why?

6. Have you and your spouse ever discussed and agreed to the nonnegotiable values you want to practice in your marriage? If so, what are they? If not, are you willing to have that discussion?

7. How would your marriage look if you agreed to practice values that made it more solid? Describe how it would change.

8. What is the single greatest obstacle preventing you from consistently living the values you desire to embrace? How can you overcome it?

PRACTICE 6

Evict the Elephant

When I was four years old, my dad came home on Halloween wearing a gorilla costume. But I had no idea it was him. I was four, so I saw a real gorilla. I was terrified. The moment he walked through the door is sealed in my memory for all time. I ran up the stairs of our rented duplex and hid in the closet. Dad came running after me, calling to me in his normal voice. But I didn't put his voice and the gorilla together, so I stayed hidden. When the door to the closet opened, I closed my eyes, thinking, *If I do not open my eyes and see the gorilla, he won't be able to see me.*

Obviously, closing my eyes and pretending didn't hide me or make the gorilla disappear. But that's how you think when you're a small child. It's children's nature to pretend. Usually it's harmless, or beneficial when you're a kid as a way to stoke creativity. But pretending is not good when you're an adult, especially if you're pretending your problems don't exist.

The Fine Family

You know where this is going. There's a phrase for disregarding a big problem. It's called ignoring the elephant in the room. Imagine if a real elephant walked into your living room with your family, and you pretended not to notice. Or if a six-ton animal sauntered into your place of business, and you just kept your head down and continued working. The only place where that might make sense is the zoo. Yet that's what we often do in our marriages and families. A huge elephant of a problem wreaks havoc on our household, blasting our ears with its trumpeting and assaulting our noses with its pooping, and we pretend it's not there. The absurdity of it reminds me of a cartoon I once saw where an elephant is lying on a psychiatrist's couch and lamenting, "Sometimes even if I stand in the middle of the room, no one acknowledges me!"

Stand-up comedian Sebastian Maniscalco did a bit in his 2019 tour "Stay Hungry" about how some families deal with their issues—or rather how they *don't*. As an example, he said his family never acknowledged that his grandfather had one leg shorter than the other because of polio. "Nobody said nothing."

I asked my father one day, "What's wrong with Grandpa?"

"What do you mean what's wrong? Why would you say that about your grandfather? What do you mean what's wrong with him?"

"I don't know, he's got a two-by-four nailed to his heel."

My family culture wasn't identical to Maniscalco's, but we ignored our elephants in the same way his did. When I was growing up, we knew not to say anything about them. Often on the way to church, my dad would lose his temper in the car (in a way somewhat less than Christlike) as we drove into the parking lot and growl, "Every one of you better put on a happy face. We're at church!"

And we did. We learned to pretend that everything was fine. We became the Fine Family. We put all our efforts into trying to *look* better than we actually *lived*. And we never addressed our real problems. We ignored the temper tantrums. The fights between Mom and Dad. The yelling and the cursing. The violence. The financial mismanagement, poor work ethic, pornography, adultery, and hypocrisy.

What a great strategy! Pretense! Pretending an issue doesn't exist always works! If you ignore the elephant, he goes away. If you close your eyes like a four-year-old, it solves the problem. If you don't talk about the elephant, you'll be fine. Right? Nope. Our elephants never went away. And we were not fine. We were deeply broken.

> We put all our efforts into trying to *look* better than we actually *lived*.

I'm not attacking my parents or my family. Lord knows I'm not good enough to condemn anyone else. What I'm saying is that *pretense* kills. Ignoring problems and being silent about them is a death sentence to a marriage—and to a family. My parents divorced when I was in middle school. Our family pretense ruined my early life. And if you don't deal with it, pretense might ruin yours.

Two Lives

Everyone has problems. Some are big and some are small. Some are thrust upon us, while others we bring on ourselves. And it doesn't matter whether or not you're a believer. If you ignore your elephants, they will cause destruction. This was true for our friend Paul, who tells his story here:

I came to faith as a middle schooler. Along with my friends Billy and Jerry, I walked down the church aisle, accepted Jesus as my savior, and was baptized later that year. Of course, at thirteen, my experience with sin was pretty rudimentary: a stray cuss word here, a girlie magazine there, the occasional rebellious attitude toward my parents. Pretty common stuff.

By my midtwenties, I was married to Amy and traveling every week for business with a Diners Club card in my pocket and too much time on my hands in big city hotels. Before long I started living two lives. When I was traveling, I was drinking uncontrollably, and during the blackouts that ensued, I was unfaithful to my wife multiple times.

I would come home from the road, ask God to wash the sin away, and play the part of the good dad, the good husband, the Christian churchgoer, the guy who had it all together. I was living in pretense. Then seven years into my marriage, with two young kids, the thin veil of lies and closely guarded secrets came crashing down.

Though I'd broken Amy's heart, she chose to stay with me. It was a gut-wrenching process of clearing the wreckage and building a new marriage from scratch. We both worked really hard and committed to a process bigger than ourselves, and we entrusted our family's future to God. We had nothing to hold on to except our shared faith, precarious as it may have been at the time. After a few years, a degree of what we considered normal returned. As an outward sign of our new marriage covenant, we decided to try for a third child and succeeded.

In my forties my career gained more traction, and I was soon an owner in my company. I was working eighty-plus hours a week, with travel, and though I'm not sure I could have seen it at the time, I now see that money, prestige, and possessions had a death grip on me. Meanwhile, my kids were growing up, and I was too busy with work to spend time with them. And all the while we were part of a great church that taught strong family values. I told myself I was being a good provider, as if providing was only a financial thing and didn't include being there spiritually, relationally, and emotionally.

Because of my distance, Amy became discouraged and depressed. This time the pretending was on her side, and she was unfaithful. I turned to alcohol again and spent some days in rehab. We experienced a second total breakdown. With a deep sense of setback, we were forced to confess that pretense had insidiously returned to our marriage and had attempted to take us out.

Shaken once again to the core, we each begged God to help us. The road back this time around was far more difficult and painful. We worked long and hard with a marriage counselor. We had to learn skills that would allow us to live in the same house without killing each other or damaging our children. It often felt like we weren't making any progress at all.

During this time I experienced a profound leading of the Holy Spirit. I was introduced to a novel by Francine Rivers titled *Redeeming Love*.[1] It was set in the Old West and used the Old Testament story of the prophet Hosea and his prostitute wife, Gomer, as its story line. No matter how badly the main character's wife treated him, the husband demonstrated a godly kind of love and forgiveness that defied logic. This love eventually won her heart, but not without a massive amount of hurt along the way. Through this book I sensed God saying to me, *Demonstrate to your wife what* my love *for her is like. Be the incarnation of my love for her.*

The Holy Spirit prompted me and showed me daily the ways I was to behave and the ways I was to react and, in many cases, how not to react. Truthfully, the path back to a marriage without pretense was pretty rough. We learned that *on* the path was truth and *off* the path was pretense.

We've now been married more than thirty years. We've since learned that in the midst of our breakdown, neither our counselor nor our pastor had much hope that our marriage would survive. But God was kind to us. I'm not saying it was or is easy. I just know that pretense doesn't work, and you have to find another way forward.

> "I sensed God saying to me, *Demonstrate to your wife what* my love *for her is like.*"

Paul and Amy are a testament to the power of God to save and heal a marriage and a family if the couple is willing to say, "There's an elephant in the room. Let's learn how to get rid of it."

The King of Elephants

David is one of the most impressive figures in Scripture. Chosen by God to be the king of Israel when he was only a teenager, he was famous for taking down Goliath with a sling and stone. He became a seasoned warrior and was celebrated for winning numerous battles for the nation of Israel. He wrote many of the psalms. He was wise, wealthy, and loved by his people. He was called a man after God's own heart, and his ancestral line produced Jesus, the Messiah, who the angel Gabriel said would sit on the throne of David (Luke 1:32). That is an amazing résumé.

Do you know what's equally amazing? The repeated breakdowns in David's life caused by pretense. The elephants in David's life created lasting family dysfunction and heartache. Here's an example: "In the spring, at the time when kings go off to war, David sent Joab out with the king's men and the whole Israelite army. They destroyed the Ammonites and besieged Rabbah. But David remained in Jerusalem" (2 Sam. 11:1). David was called and anointed to be the king of Israel. His job was to lead the nation's army into battle when there was trouble. But what did he do this time? He stayed home. David had been serving as king for fifteen or twenty years, so he should have known better. It was his duty to lead his warriors, yet he didn't go out to fight with them. Why? Scripture doesn't say.

Was David getting weary of serving God? Was the personal cost of going to war becoming too much to bear? Was he getting soft? Who wants to go live in a tent and endure the elements when they can enjoy all the pleasures of the palace?

Was it pride? Had David gotten used to God's blessing and forgotten that victory came at God's hand? Was he pretending that he was no longer responsible for keeping his own zeal aflame?

Was David a victim of boredom? Had the business of besieging cities become dull, tedious, repetitive, monotonous? Did he expect other warriors to be passionate for the kingdom while he was casual? Or had David been looking down from his roof for quite some time and planning an indulgent escapade after he had sent his warriors to war?

No matter what the cause, David told himself a lie: the king can stay home in wartime. He gave himself an option he shouldn't have. It was self-deception. It probably seemed small, maybe even innocent. But let's tell it like it is: David let an elephant into the palace.

David's pretense that he didn't need to fulfill his duty as king led to what is described in 2 Samuel 11:2–5:

One evening David got up from his bed and walked around on the roof of the palace. From the roof he saw a woman bathing. The woman was very beautiful, and David sent someone to find out about her. The man said, "She is Bathsheba, the daughter of Eliam and the wife of Uriah the Hittite." Then David sent messengers to get her. She came to him, and he slept with her. (Now she was purifying herself from her monthly uncleanness.) Then she went back home. The woman conceived and sent word to David, saying, "I am pregnant."

Irresponsibility led to adultery. And if that's not enough, David went on to cover up the adultery and pregnancy by having Bathsheba's husband, Uriah, killed. On top of that, he later made Bathsheba his wife, as if he were nobly marrying the widow of one of his fallen mighty men to provide for her.

David lied to himself, he lied to Bathsheba's family, he lied to the nation, and he lied to God.

Did David think failing to go to war at the time kings were supposed to would cause him to violate four of the ten commandments: don't lie, don't covet, don't commit adultery, don't murder? Probably not. But that's the insidious nature of pretending. "It will be fine," we tell ourselves, and we open the door to the elephant.

That's not the only example of pretense in David's life. David had multiple wives (a topic for a whole other book), and so he had many children by different mothers. How could that dynamic *not* cause problems? It's like having a herd of elephants. But David ignored them too.

The worst family problem occurred between the children of two of David's wives. Absalom and his sister Tamar, the children of one wife, were physically beautiful. And Amnon, David's son by another wife, lusted after his half-sister Tamar. He came up with an elaborate deception to be alone with her, and when he was, he raped her. He then rejected and disgraced her. It's a gut-wrenching story. But what's equally horrific and stunningly unjust is that when David heard about it, he did nothing! It's as though a giant, ugly, destructive elephant broke into the palace and started wrecking his family, and the mighty warrior-king David ignored it.

When David ignored the catastrophe and failed to take action, Absalom decided to do something about it himself. He waited and plotted for *two* years, deceiving everyone into thinking that all was well. Then one day he hosted a party for all the king's sons, including Amnon, and commanded his men to kill him. This may all sound like a modern bloody revenge movie, but it was David's actual dysfunctional family.

David's family was not fine. Paul's family was not fine. My family when I was growing up was not fine. And if you have elephants living in your marriage or family, you are not fine either. If you don't evict your elephants, your marriage and your family *will* suffer. They may even be destroyed.

Evict, Don't Adopt

Have you ever seen vehicles with stickers of stick-figure families on the back? They were very popular a few years ago. Each member of a family is represented, right on down to the cat and dog. During the height of their popularity, we created stickers like those to hand out to anyone at the church who wanted them, but in our version, instead of a dog or cat, the family pet was an elephant. It was our tongue-in-cheek way of saying that we make family pets out of the elephants in our lives, when we need to learn to evict them instead.

Family Life?

If you're ready to evict your elephants, instead of treating them like members of the family, you need to do three things.

1. EVICT THE ELEPHANT INWARDLY

At its core, pretense is rooted in deception. But before deception enters into a marriage, family, business, church, community, or nation, it privately resides in a person. We deceive ourselves. We lie to ourselves. We tell ourselves things will be fine to avoid problems or pain or discipline or responsibility or reality we don't want to face. This self-deception is deeply destructive.

Before David lied to God or anyone else, he lied to himself. At any point he could have stopped and said, "I'm lying to myself. I'm pretending it's okay for a leader of a nation to stay home while his men fight the war. I'm pretending I have options I do not have." Staying home is not an option when you're king. Having an affair with a married woman is not an option for a follower of God. Nor is lying, cheating, or murdering. David could have stopped living in pretense. The moment he saw Bathsheba naked from his roof, he could have said, "I shouldn't even be here. If I were where I am supposed to be, I would never have seen her. Get me my armor and my horse! I'm off to Rabbah to join the siege."

Pretense is *never* the right option. Pretending the temper outburst never happened is not going to bring harmony to the family. Cleaning up after the person who makes emotional messes and never owns them or apologizes for them isn't going to bring peace. Ignoring the irresponsible credit card binge that blows the budget isn't going to improve the situation. The snide comments, the name-calling, the broken promises, the silent treatment, the passive-aggressive behavior are all elephants. When you don't deal with them, you're opening the door to let them into your house. You're making them your family pets. Never believe the lies of pretense that say:

If you ignore the elephant, he will go away.
If we don't talk about the elephant, we'll be fine.

> Pretense is one of the most unrecognized and destructive forces in our lives.

No, the elephant isn't going away on its own. And, no, you're not going to be fine. You're going to be up to your nose in what elephants produce.

Pretense is one of the most unrecognized and destructive forces in our lives. If you want to be truly happy in life and marriage, you'll have to get past it. And that starts by evicting the elephants in your heart and soul. You have to say to yourself, "I have a problem, and I'm going to stop pretending I don't."

2. EVICT THE ELEPHANT OUTWARDLY

To truly get rid of the elephant, you need to go to your spouse or your family and say, "There's an elephant in the room with us, and we need to deal with it to have a better, richer, happier life." Because that never happened in my family while I was growing up, I have a lifetime of wounds and sorrows caused by our pretense. And I brought that whole herd of elephants into my marriage. Marcia brought a few of her own as well. We're sure you did too. Even if by some miracle you didn't, marriage is complex enough and difficult enough that some elephants will come find you. And if you don't evict them, they will set themselves up as your pets.

You may not know how to evict an elephant from your marriage. But if you have told yourself the truth about its existence, you have started the eviction process internally. If you begin talking with your spouse about it, you will be on your way to getting that elephant out of the house. But you'll need to take one more step to complete the process.

3. SOLVE PROBLEMS ONE SHOVELFUL AT A TIME

When I was in college, Mr. Byron, a friend who was a high school principal, shared a personal experience I've never forgotten. He decided to work on a major landscape renovation in his backyard. Motivated by his big vision and enthusiasm, he ordered a large load of dirt for his do-it-yourself landscape project. When a dump truck showed up, backed onto his driveway, and left a huge mountain of dirt in the middle of it, he was overwhelmed. "What am I going to do?" he asked himself. "I can't move all that dirt!"

After a few days of paralysis, he came up with an answer: "I can move it one shovelful at a time." So that's what he did. For the next four months, he kept at it. He transformed his backyard one shovelful at a time.

I have applied that process to many of my problems ever since I heard his story. Many of the problems in marriage and family can feel huge. When we finally stop pretending and face them, they can look like a mountain of elephant manure, something more than we believe we can handle. And we feel deeply discouraged as a result. If that describes you, then perhaps Mr. Byron's plan of attack will be helpful. Don't try to clean up the whole thing at once. Just evict the elephant and handle the mess one shovelful at a time.

The longer the elephant has lived with you and the more destructive it's been, the more shoveling you will need to do. The process will definitely feel like a B Zone. But you *can* get to the bottom of the pile as long as you don't Q Zone. You already know the steps. So focus on the C-Zone rewards of an evicted elephant. Get your hands up in prayer about it. Then start calling for the fair fights needed to take care of the pile one shovelful at a time. Once you've resolved one issue, move on to the next. And the next. You can do it. With every issue you resolve, you will be that much closer to having a clean, healthy, and functioning family.

Evicting Everyday Elephants

Some of the elephants people deal with are pretty common in marriage. Others are rare. Whether they come from your past or they simply show up uninvited, the process of dealing with them is always the same: evict inwardly, evict outwardly, shovel the problem. For some elephants, that process might take a few hours. Others may take a *decade* to permanently evict. You may be thinking, *A decade? Really?* It takes as long as it takes. No matter how long that is, the work will be worth it. Why? Because an ignored elephant will never go away, and the poop will keep piling up. When you live with an elephant, you're not only weighed down by the problem, but you're also exhausted by pretending it's not there. It's miserable.

That kind of pretense is one of the reasons our married life was so difficult in the early years. Marcia and I pretended we didn't have any elephants in our marriage. We lived our lives, did our jobs, led our church, all while ignoring our elephants, believing that they would go away by themselves. We both thought we'd be fine by being silent about them. But we weren't. So we finally decided that as hard as it was to talk about them, we needed to evict them.

We want to share six of the common elephants that couples face in marriage. Many of them Marcia and I had to deal with. We hope you will recognize the ones negatively affecting you as a couple and decide to promptly take care of them.

1. MONEY

Let's deal with the biggest elephant first, the one that can weigh twelve tons. Did you even know an elephant could get that big? (That's the record holder: a 24,000-pound bull elephant in Angola in 1956 that measured thirteen feet tall at the shoulder.) For many couples, money is their biggest elephant in the room.

Marcia and I have had plenty of elephant moments related to

money. We hope sharing our money issues will help you start to address yours.

MARCIA: I grew up in a solid Christian, traditional home, the kind of home where my dad worked and my mom stayed home and took care of the kids. My dad took care of the family finances, and my mom would spend what my dad told her she could spend. I would not say we were well-to-do, but we also didn't lack for anything. So, for me, money was neutral. I just assumed it would always be there when I needed it. No big deal.

KEVIN: I grew up in a dysfunctional home. My dad had difficulty keeping work and even more trouble managing money. Both my parents were high school dropouts because Mom got pregnant in the eleventh grade. By the time they were twenty, they had their third child, me. After they divorced, when I was in middle school, we never recovered financially. Mom, my sister, and I lived on food stamps in government-subsidized housing during my high school years. And I was penniless in college.

MARCIA: I married Kevin after my sophomore year of college, so I never lived on my own. I didn't have the experience of paying for a car, a place to live, the utilities, or any other expenses. I went from my dad taking care of the finances to my husband taking care of the finances. And I kept thinking the money would always be there.

KEVIN: It never occurred to me that no one had ever taught me how to manage money. Going into adulthood, I had no skills. This almost guaranteed that we would always spend everything we earned and be forever poor. When I did eventually learn, it was from books by people such as Ron Blue, and I discovered that our family did almost everything wrong when it came to money. I had to learn to think completely differently about money and learn to live by a budget.

MARCIA: We were fine as a family until I quit teaching to raise our children. Without my income, money began to get a lot tighter. The church was not doing as well as we had expected, so that wasn't making the situation any better. I could see what was happening, but I still acted like money would always be there. Deep down I knew it couldn't be, but I chose to have an optimistic attitude. I kept pretending that things would get better soon.

KEVIN: I probably had to confront my own internal elephant first. I was always trying to put an optimistic spin on our financial situation by saying, "Everything will be fine." But facts defied my optimism. The more I owned the truth about our family's money situation, the more I realized we were in trouble. The reality was that we were living like I had when I was growing up. We kept spending up to our limits, and every time we had a little more money, we spent a little more.

If we're honest with ourselves—and this is where evicting the elephant starts—this is probably the first elephant most couples need to evict. We want options and possessions we simply can't afford. We want more technology, more toys, more meals out, more fun experiences, and we spend more money—even money we don't have—to get them. As a result, we stop honoring God financially, we give less to others, and we end up with no savings or margin. That's the elephant I finally came face-to-face with. And while I was dealing with it for the first time, that is when Marcia wanted to add a third child to our family.

MARCIA: When I talked to Kevin about having a third child, the biggest hurdle for him was financial. He said we couldn't afford another child. Even though the church was finally growing, and we were earning a little more, he didn't want to be under the kind of financial pressure that another child would bring. I argued that another child wouldn't cost that much. We already had the basics, and kids don't eat much. We could just tighten our belts.

KEVIN: As you know, I disagreed. Strongly. The medical costs would tank us. The kids' health issues would surprise us. With food and diapers, our expenses would rise. Plus our three-bedroom home would be too small, as would our car.

MARCIA: We went back and forth on the money issue, with Kevin saying that I was not facing reality and me saying that it was all going to be okay. I thought the money would be there when we needed it. It was just a matter of time.

Even though we did the annual budget together, Kevin managed our money and paid the bills. To have a meeting of the minds, I did the books for a season, even though I didn't have a knack for it. I knew that if I was going to understand the pressure, I'd have to carry the pressure. I was secretly confident I could show Kevin how to live within a budget.

Boy, was I wrong! There was simply no way to easily make ends meet. Often they didn't. The budget was super-tight, so when one thing went wrong, which it always did, the whole thing fell apart. My eyes were opened. I could no longer live in my pretend world of "everything will be all right" and "the money will always be there."

KEVIN: The surprising benefit of all of this was not an "I told you so." It was a new partnership regarding money.

MARCIA: It was the best thing that could have happened. I realized that money was a real thing and couldn't be taken for granted. And when we had money shortages anytime after that, we faced them together, honestly and openly.

How are you and your spouse when it comes to dealing with money? Is there an elephant in the room? Are you both on the same page? Do you both know your situation? Do you talk about it? Do you both agree on how to handle it? If both of you can't answer all of those questions, you probably have an elephant you need to deal with.

2. ESCAPING

We hinted at this elephant in practice 1 when we talked about people checking out on their marriage when they're stuck in the

B Zone. That was one of the issues with Paul and Amy. The first time their marriage broke down, it was because Paul was escaping through alcohol, which led to other breakdowns, including infidelity. The second time it was because he was engaged with his business instead of his family. In response, Amy escaped through an affair. King David was doing the same thing when he failed to go to war. That escape led to his further escape to adultery.

Sometimes *escape* is the elephant. Other times it is the result of an elephant. But each of us needs to ask ourselves these questions:

- Am I failing to show up anywhere I have responsibilities or commitments?
- Am I disengaged or distracted in my marriage?
- Am I failing to show up for my kids?
- Am I distracting myself at work?
- Am I neglecting my faith?
- Am I playing video games for hours?
- Am I spending to make myself feel better?
- Am I eating when I'm feeling sad?

If the answer to any of these questions is yes, the next question is why. You can evict the elephant inwardly only when you acknowledge it's there.

3. HEALTH AND FITNESS

That is an easy lead-in to another common elephant: health and fitness. Marcia and I both care about physical fitness, but in truth, I've had a harder time keeping fit after age thirty than Marcia has.

She has always maintained her college weight and size. It's taken effort, but she's done it. I, on the other hand, gained over forty pounds after college, and my weight has been a challenge ever since. My problem: I don't merely eat to live. I live to eat!

After I gained weight, it soon became clear that it was unfair for me to pretend there was no elephant in the room. I had to face my elephant, evict it inwardly, then evict it outwardly with Marcia, and from time to time even publicly with the church. Eventually, I fought to lose thirty pounds. However, I tend to be up and down in my personality, and that affects my weight. So I cycle up and down by about ten pounds, unlike Marcia, who is very steady.

If you are the person in your marriage who battles overeating and maintaining a healthy lifestyle, don't make your spouse the one who has to bring up this elephant. Be the one to evict the elephant first inside yourself to serve your spouse as well as yourself.

4. BOUNDARIES

Every successful marriage has good boundaries. They help keep couples away from moral failures as well as give them the security that comes from having trust in their relationship. Here is how Marcia and I have worked to keep this elephant out of our marriage.

MARCIA: One of the common elephants in marriage is jeal-
ousy. It's usually viewed negatively, but it can also have
a positive impact. God himself says he is jealous when
we give sacred love that is due only to him to someone or something else [Ex. 34:14]. We demonstrate
our love for him by putting him first in our lives. In a

marriage, we demonstrate our love for our spouse by putting them first and giving them no cause to doubt our love.

Kevin is outgoing and gregarious. I think he can unknowingly cross the line into unintentional flirting that could give another woman the wrong idea. At the same time, Kevin has noticed men at my work who he believed were making moves on me.

So we made boundaries an open, safe conversation. If either of us notices the other might be giving the wrong impression to someone, we point it out, not as an accusation, but as a warning. We also admitted that since we are humanly capable of being attracted to another person, we would talk about it. We identified what types of people are attractive to us, and we agreed that we would give them a wide berth. That way we could never get close to those types of people.

These very frank conversations about healthy boundaries can be challenging, but they are important if you want to experience a good, lasting, deep relationship and the Second Happy that comes from it.

5. BOREDOM

Life can make you feel like you're in a rut. So can marriage. Rather than let the elephant of boredom enter the room and suck all the air out of your marriage, admit to it and work through the cycles of relational boredom that anyone can find themselves in.

There are a lot of ways to do that. It might mean mixing up your date-night routine, making fresh goals together, planning vacations, shifting hobbies so you can do some together, working on a project you both care about, reading the same book and discussing it, taking in a concert, going on long walks or hikes, or working out together. Whatever it takes to stay connected and break up the monotony can be a good thing.

Listen, it's a lie to suggest that any relationship should not take work, and that includes marriage. Everything worthwhile takes effort, energy, and intentionality. The reward is an elephant-free companionship. And by the way, *incompatibility* is near the top of the list of reasons people say they get divorced. Incompatibility doesn't develop all of a sudden. Often it starts with boredom, and then develops because of neglect. So when boredom threatens, end it before it becomes a real problem.

> It's a lie to suggest that any relationship should not take work, and that includes marriage.

6. SEX

We began this list of common marital elephants with money. We're going to end it with sex, the other big one. Let's start with God's perspective on the subject. If you are a follower of Christ, you have only one person with whom you get to share the God-given pleasure of sex: your spouse. The guidelines in 1 Corinthians 7:2–5 are clear:

Each man should have sexual relations with his own wife, and each woman with her own husband. The husband should fulfill his marital duty to his wife, and likewise the wife to her husband. The wife does not have authority over her own body but yields it to her husband. In the same way, the husband does not have authority over his own body but yields it to his wife. Do not deprive each other except perhaps by mutual consent and for a time, so that you may devote yourselves to prayer. Then come together again so that Satan will not tempt you because of your lack of self-control.

KEVIN: One of the standing jokes I tell the congregation is "I am Marcia's jungle gym. You might feel bad for her, but *this* [pointing to my less-than-perfect body] is her only option." They laugh and so do I. But the sacredness of the marriage bed is really no laughing matter. Sexually, neither Marcia nor I have other options. Not adultery, not emotional affairs, not online flirting, not lusting after pornography.

Because you have only one option sexually—each other—the subject of sex needs to be an open conversation between you. Both of you need to talk about how you initiate sex, how you experience it, and how often you expect to share it. To be blunt, marriages that experience the Second Happy must become elephant-free in the bedroom.

You think this would be easy, but it's not. You might be amazed at how huge a problem this is for many, if not most, couples. The elephant can show up on either side of the bed, and it's often very difficult for couples to deal with it.

Given the world we live in, this is a battleground for many

marriages. That was certainly true for Andrew and Liz. I met with Andrew when he was in college, and we talked about his dating life. Since then, he has graduated, gotten married, and become a dad. Here's the story of their struggles in this area:

I met Liz through mutual friends at an event. My goodness! She was beautiful, smart, funny, and playful. It took me a few weeks to work up the courage to ask her out. Our dating relationship grew quickly from there. Within the year we were engaged, and within two years we were married.

But the honeymoon phase faded quickly, and we found ourselves with a child on the way. We pretended we had a good marriage, but we didn't. It was bad. We fought constantly, lacked intimacy, and couldn't figure out what was going on. Honestly, I hadn't expected Liz to *complete* me, but I had at the very least expected her to be *compatible* with me. It was in this season that I found myself wondering, *Where did I go wrong? Did I marry the wrong person?*

As we've said, when the honeymoon happiness fades, and we're faced with the reality of making a marriage work, most of us feel this way. We wonder if we've made a mistake. And for many couples, the elephant of an unfulfilling sex life is a major source of their unhappiness.

Now back to Andrew and Liz.

Like so many people in their twenties, I was looking at marriage to be the answer to my problems. I learned quickly that marriage doesn't solve problems; it exposes them. I began to realize that our lack of intimacy wasn't a problem that we had *formed in* our marriage, but a problem that we had *brought into* our marriage. We had been pretending that past relationships hadn't followed us into our relationship.

In the beginning of my young adult years, I was in a dating relationship with someone with whom I could be myself, and it grew serious. When it came to dating, I knew there were lines you were not supposed to cross. I grew up in church and had heard the same words everyone else has heard: "Don't have sex before you get married." But as that relationship progressed, my ability to justify crossing that line became easier and easier. I told myself, *Well, we love each other. We are going to get married anyway. This feels right.* Soon we were crossing that line.

For the four years we were together, I acted as if we were married, but we weren't. What I hadn't realized was that while pretending to be married, I was actually merging two hearts to become one. When the relationship came to an unexpected and devastating end, I found myself bouncing around from one dating relationship to another, seeking the oneness I had known before. It made me realize that sexual sin is like a river with a calm surface but a deadly undertow. It seems to be safe enough to play in, but when you jump in, it will pull you under and sweep you away. I had taken lightly what God does not, and by the time I discovered that, it was too late; the damage had been done.

During our engagement, Liz and I had a candid conversation about our past dating relationships. She had also crossed the line with other men. We both had baggage that we brought into the marriage, but what we underestimated was how far it would follow us and how much damage it would cause. Our past actions had formed a selfishness inside our souls that we expected the other person to fix. As a result:

- We expected oneness but experienced distance.
- We expected intimacy but experienced what felt like one-night stands.
- We expected fullness but experienced emptiness.
- We expected happiness but experienced discontentment.

That caused us to be more like roommates than soul mates. We not only needed forgiveness, we needed healing.

By having sex with others before they were married, Andrew and Liz never dreamed that they were opening a door for an elephant in their lives. They never would have believed that the elephant would follow them into their marriage and do so much damage.

> "Sexual sin is like a river with a calm surface but a deadly undertow."

In our culture, this is one of the most common difficulties couples face. Their pasts follow them into their bedrooms and create problems. Often they don't want to admit—even to themselves—that their previous sexual activity is hurting their marriage. Many don't have the self-awareness or the courage to evict the elephants inwardly. And if they can't or won't do this internally, they can't deal with them outwardly with their spouse. Fortunately, Andrew and Liz identified their elephants. Andrew said,

Through prayer, I finally came to a place where I asked God for forgiveness. The beautiful truth about the grace of God is that he did and does forgive me through Jesus. But what people fail to talk about is that while forgiveness removes the eternal consequences of sin, it doesn't remove all the earthly consequences. It took years of counseling, honest conversations, and prayer for God to heal us and our marriage.

With three kids and almost a decade of marriage under our belt, Liz and I continually keep the conversation going about where our marriage is. To be perfectly transparent, our marriage is better, but it isn't perfect.

No marriage is perfect. Marcia and mine isn't. Neither is yours. But every marriage can be better. And any marriage can become elephant-free. You just need to stop the pretense, be willing to take an honest look at yourself, and look for any elephants. When you find one, confront it internally. Ask yourself what you may be doing to feed the elephant and make it your pet, instead of evicting it. Then talk to your spouse about it. Getting any issue out into the open is a *great* first step. Never underestimate that. Then work through the issues, one shovel at a time.

If you've been married for more than six months, there are elephants in the room with you. Do something about them. If you've been married for a long time and never had any difficult conversations with each other about money, escaping, health and fitness, boundaries, boredom, or sex, you're living with a whole herd of elephants. It's time to deal with them, one at a time, shovelful by shovelful. And don't even think about going to the Q Zone on your marriage because of them. If you get divorced and start over, you will take *all* of your old elephants with you into your new relationship, *plus* you'll have to take on your new partner's elephants as well.

Andrew told us, "God has been kind to us in this process, but it required us to stop pretending and start praying and talking. Where we experienced distance, we are now experiencing oneness. We would say there is hope for anyone who quits pretending and trusts God in marriage."

They did it, Marcia and I did it, and so can you.

CONVERSATION FOR A COUPLE

Answer these questions on your own, with your spouse doing the same. Then make an appointment with each other to discuss your answers. Have an honest conversation with the goal of serving each other in order to develop a better marriage. Be honest with your feelings, but focus on how *you* can change by applying the practice described to yourself, not your spouse.

1. Which of the six elephants listed in the practice are issues in your marriage: money, escaping, health and fitness, boundaries, boredom, or sex? List all that apply.

2. How do each of the elephants you identified negatively affect your relationship with your spouse or children?

3. Which elephant do you want to deal with first? What must you do to evict it inwardly?

4. How can you deal with the elephant outwardly by discussing it with your spouse? Write out the problem as you see it, including how you negatively contribute to it.

Once you've shared your answers, discuss what each of you needs to do as a result of your conversation.

DISCUSSION FOR A SMALL GROUP

1. Who was your favorite pet? If you never had a pet, explain why.

2. What subjects were taboo in your family when you were growing up? Why?

3. How did your family of origin deal with difficult issues? Describe it. What practices have you taken into your own family?

4. Why do you think couples pretend they don't have problems, instead of identifying them and working on them together? Name as many reasons as you can.

5. What does pretense do to a marriage? A family?

6. What have been the greatest obstacles to you for evicting the elephants in your marriage or family?

7. How would your marriage improve if you could evict the elephants and live completely without pretense?

8. Did you and your spouse discuss your answers to the "Conversation for a Couple" questions? How did that go? Are you willing to start working on the problems one shovelful at a time? When will you start?

PRACTICE 7

Choose Your Bucket Wisely

Just out of college, I was hired as an assistant pastor at a three-year-old church in Kentwood, Michigan, by my longtime friend and senior pastor Wayne Schmidt. A few weeks later, Marcia and I were married. At that time, Marcia was finishing her degree in music education and needed a job, so Wayne hired her as a part-time secretary in the office.

Newlyweds working together. What could be more romantic? Not only would we be home together, but we would work together too! (Cue the romantic music and the sounds of birds chirping.) We'd ride together to the office. Perhaps we could have a picnic lunch in the park every day. We'd be the picture-perfect couple. Then reality hit. Only a few days into our new jobs, we had an interaction that each of us remembers somewhat differently.

KEVIN: It was a beautiful fall day in Michigan. I strolled into
Marcia's quaint office and politely, kindly requested,
"Marcia, darling, I'm working on this project and need

to follow up with several people so I can find out if they are planning to be part of this event. Here's a list of people I'd like to ask you to call for me. It would be ever so helpful if I had that information in a couple of days. Thank you so much. I'm so glad we get to be together every minute. Love you!"

But that's not how she remembers it.

MARCIA: It was a beautiful fall day in Michigan. Kevin rushed into my cramped little office space and demanded that I do *his* work for him. "Marcia," he barked, "I have an endless list of phone calls I need to make, but I do not have the inclination or the time to make them. I know you hate making phone calls, but, hey, I'm your boss. So here you go." And he tossed the list on my desk. "Get to it. I need it done yesterday!"

While we don't agree on how the interaction started or whose memory is more accurate, we both agree on what happened next.

MARCIA: "You know I hate to make phone calls. Why would you ask me to do that?"

KEVIN: "Um, because it's your *job* and I need it done."

MARCIA: "Well, it's actually *your* job, not mine. And I'm not going to do it!"

KEVIN: "But it *is* your job. And you work for me. So you have to do what I *tell* you to do!"

MARCIA: "No, I don't work for you. Technically, I work for Pastor Wayne, and *you* can't tell me what to do!"

KEVIN: "Technically, you are the church secretary, and I'm now a real-deal pastor at this church. So you *do* work for me. And you *do* have to do what I tell you to do!"

MARCIA: "I'm your *wife*, and you don't tell me what to *do*!"

KEVIN: "I'm not telling you what to do as my wife. I'm telling you what to do as my *secretary*. And you will *do* it!"

MARCIA: "I'm your wife first, and you know I hate making calls. I will only do what Wayne tells me to do."

You can probably guess how this ended. I put my foot down. I told her how it was really going to be at work. And then I went back to my office and made all the calls myself.

That's the day we decided we could live together, but we could not work together. And we agreed we never would. However, having been married for thirty-seven years beyond that interaction, we can now say from the benefit of experience that we were wrong. The issue wasn't that we couldn't work together. The problem was that we took a small spark of conflict, an irritation, and we both poured gasoline on it, creating an explosion.

Everyone Has Two Buckets

I don't know exactly when, but early in my career as a pastor, I heard John Maxwell teach a concept that I've often used in my marriage, family, leadership, and church. It's a simple concept, but I think it is one of the clearest pictures and the most profound practices for developing and maintaining healthy relationships. John, who also included this in his book *Developing the Leaders Around You*,[1] eventually became a kind mentor and a gracious friend.

Here's the concept. Imagine that everyone carries around two buckets in life. Every day. Everywhere. One bucket contains gasoline and the other contains water. How you use those buckets will either build things up or burn things down in your life. This idea has transformed my life and my marriage. And its value has only increased over the years. Marcia and I believe that if you choose your bucket wisely, it will not only build your marriage but will change your life.

While this concept is true for all relationships, we'll talk about it in the context of marriage. Whenever a problem arises—a spark of disagreement, an ember of anger, a flame of offense—when you respond, you choose one of the two buckets and pour it on the problem. If you choose the water bucket, you extinguish the flames and stop the fire. If you choose the gasoline bucket, you turn that small spark into a raging, destructive fire. That's all there is to it. In a window of time as brief as two seconds, you make a choice of which bucket to use.

> In a window of
> time as brief as
> two seconds,
> you make a
> choice of which
> bucket to use.

That day at the office in the early weeks of our marriage, each of us poured gasoline on a simple spark. If we had understood the buckets, if we had possessed greater humility and maturity, we could have wisely doused the embers instead of building a bonfire. When Marcia said, "You know I hate to make phone calls. Why would you ask me to do that?" instead of saying, "Because it's your *job*," I could have said, "I know you hate making calls. I'm sorry. But this other urgent task is something I *have* to do, so I need your help. Both are important to the church. Would you please help me by doing as many calls as you can?"

Just to prove that we were the problem—and it had nothing to do with our ability to work together—Marcia recently started working for me. I kid you not. She recently accepted the role of research assistant to the senior pastor. She was already a great music teacher and mom, and now, with her seminary degree, she's really good at what she does. And when we work together, I never tell her what to do, and she always does what I ask. See the difference? Oh, and I still make my own phone calls!

When Sparks Fly

Almost anything can start a fire in your marriage. It can be something as small as a misunderstanding, an unkind word, an unmet expectation, or even some imaginary offenses. Or the problem can be much greater, such as broken trust, betrayal, or adultery. No matter the size of the spark, when you fight fire with fire by pouring gasoline on it, what blows up is your marriage.

We may casually use phrases such as "pouring gasoline on the fire," but do you understand what actually happens when someone really does that? I read recently about a twentysomething who put gasoline on the embers in a firepit because he wanted to restart the fire. The fiery explosion that followed seriously injured his nearby girlfriend and killed him![2] A gallon of gasoline is the explosive equivalent of twenty sticks of dynamite.[3]

We all know the difference between the two buckets and how much the outcome changes, depending on which one we use. You can even read about it throughout Scripture:

- "A soft answer [water] turns away wrath, but a harsh word [gasoline] stirs up anger." (Prov. 15:1 ESV)
- "Fools give full vent to their rage [gasoline], but the wise bring calm [water] in the end." (Prov. 29:11)
- "A hot-tempered man [gasoline] stirs up strife, but he who is slow to anger [water] quiets contention." (Prov. 15:18 ESV)
- "A man without self-control [gasoline] is like a city broken into and left without walls." (Prov. 25:28 ESV)

When we use the wrong bucket, we create destruction and chaos, which fuels malice, anger, rage, divisiveness, and bitterness in our marriage. Bitterness is especially destructive, because it can become a prison that holds us back in life. It steals our freedom and joy. It traps us in sin. And it can make us feel like victims, which only adds more fuel to the problem. It's as if Ephesians 4:29–32 was written directly to those who want to use the gasoline bucket:

> Do not let any unwholesome talk come out of your mouths, but only what is helpful for building others up according to their needs, that it may benefit those who listen. And do not grieve the Holy Spirit of God, with whom you were sealed for the day of redemption. Get rid of all bitterness, rage and anger, brawling

and slander, along with every form of malice. Be kind and compassionate to one another, forgiving each other, just as in Christ God forgave you.

If Marcia and I could convince you of one thing, it would be the power of the water bucket to calm conflict, defuse anger, prevent malice, and diminish disrespect toward each other. The power of the water bucket can revive a marriage through forgiveness. It can wash away bitterness. If you have become bitter and feel imprisoned by it, know that you hold the key to unlock the door and let yourself out whenever you choose. All it takes is a commitment to choose the right bucket.

> If you have become bitter and feel imprisoned by it, know that you hold the key to unlock the door.

How to Put Out the Fire

Colossians 3:12–15 contains the road map for how to choose the water bucket. It says,

Put on then, as God's chosen ones, holy and beloved, compassionate hearts, kindness, humility, meekness, and patience, bearing with one another and, if one has a complaint against another, forgiving each other; as the Lord has forgiven you, so you also must forgive. And above all these put on love, which binds everything together in perfect harmony. And let the peace of Christ rule in your hearts, to which indeed you were called in one body. And be thankful. (ESV)

We are to bear with one another, forgive each other, and put on love, which brings harmony. Or, as we choose to describe it: pause and put out the fire, forgive the offense, and restore the relationship. We'll discuss each in detail.

1. PAUSE AND PUT OUT THE FIRE

Learning to pause and put out a fire instead of fueling it was incredibly difficult for me. I was raised in a house of fools who vented their anger, were hot-tempered, and stirred up strife. I became a fool who wanted to blame other people for the bonfires I created, but the truth is, I had the habit of picking up the gasoline bucket and making small fires much worse. I was like an ancient city with no walls—unprotected and vulnerable to destruction—all because I lacked self-control. This is the opposite of what God wants from us. James 1:19–20 says,

> My dear brothers and sisters, take note of this: Everyone should be quick to listen, slow to speak and slow to become angry, because human anger does not produce the righteousness that God desires.

I was raised in a slow-to-hear, quick-to-speak, fast-to-anger family. In no way was the level of our tempers more evident than in the way we drove—fast and angry. Truthfully, you can learn a lot about a person's character from how they drive. Our family dynamic growing up was the opposite of "bearing with one another," and I brought that attitude into my marriage with Marcia. Here's how Marcia and I came into our marriage.

KEVIN: My dad was fast to anger and fast on the road. My two older brothers and I basically followed in those footsteps. Anger would build in my dad, and then he'd spew his temper volcanically. His fits of rage set the tone and defined our normal way of handling conflict in our home. We were expected to be godly, unless, of course, we were angry. Then we could say harsh things, use cutting words, vent frustration, curse, throw things, break things, punch walls, and threaten physical violence. After we had calmed down, we would pretend everything was fine. All the men in the house were quick to anger. And we all had the gift of speed on the road too.

MARCIA: My dad was slow to anger. With five kids born over six years you would think there would have been plenty of times my father lost his cool, but it seldom happened. The one time he was angry with me was the night I broke curfew. But that's a story for another time. Dad simply led with love instead of anger, and that was surprisingly effective as a disciplinary measure for my sister, my three brothers, and me.

Dad was slow on the road too. He had self-discipline. If the speed limit was fifty-five miles per hour, he drove fifty-five. "We'll get there," he would say. "No need to rush. The few minutes you save by speeding are not worth it. Leave a few minutes early and you won't have to break the law." For him it was a matter of honoring God.

KEVIN: I grew up fast to anger *and* fast on the road. And my infatuation with speed was shared and encouraged by my two older brothers. In the mid- to late '70s each of them custom built his own '69 Chevy Nova. Picture a high-performance muscle car with a Holley four-barrel carburetor, Cragar wheels, a slapstick shifter, a positraction rear end, and glasspack mufflers. They could play the eight-track tape of Foreigner on full blast and still not be able to make out the words to "Cold as Ice" because the sound of the engine was so loud! Whenever a traffic light turned green, they came off the line as if it were a drag race. Some of those memories still make me smile.

However, I admit, the combination of anger and automotive speed is not a good one. It can be dangerous. I remember many times riding in the back seat when one of my brothers was annoyed by another driver and he hit the gas, using high speed to make his point. More than once I thought we were about to die in an accident because of their road rage.

But that didn't happen only with my older brothers. When I got my license, I sped too. I was a card-carrying Myers and I drove like one. And in Bible college, I once lost my temper over a silly game and actually put my fist through the wall.

MARCIA: I'm slow to anger like my dad, but I am fast on the road. It's not because I love speed, but because I have a bit of a heavy foot. If the road is clear and I'm not paying attention, I tend to go over the speed limit. Kevin is fast on purpose. He loves cars and motorcycles and would prefer if he could set his own speed limit. He loves the thrill. As you can imagine, between us, we've spent a bit of money over the years on speeding tickets and increased insurance rates.

KEVIN: I'm sorry to say Marcia has had to endure my quick driving and quick temper more than a few times over the course of our marriage.

When I look back at how I used to treat people, including Marcia, I'm quite humbled. I would love to blame my temper on how I was raised. When I was young, I did. But that's really no excuse. Each of us is responsible for which bucket we choose. Even after I realized that, I can tell you it was a long and difficult journey for me to change. I had to recognize that the way I was raised wasn't right. Then I had to allow the Holy Spirit to re-parent me so I could become more like my heavenly Father, who is "gracious and compassionate, slow to anger and rich in love" (Ps. 145:8).

> I had to allow the Holy Spirit to re-parent me so I could become more like my heavenly Father.

How have I been able to do that? First,

I remind myself that Jesus rescued me from all my sin, including my temper. I ask the Holy Spirit within me to help me make decisions based on his wisdom and his values, knowing these will give me the life and marriage I long for. And every day I try to die to the way I grew up and instead to grow up in Christ. I'm still vulnerable to quick temper flare-ups, but now when anger tries to rise up in me, I intentionally pause before doing or saying anything. I take two or three seconds to calm down, let God work in me, and gain perspective. Then I pick up the water bucket. After that, I decide whether to get my hands up, pick a fair fight, take a knee, or choose some other positive course of action.

2. FORGIVE THE OFFENSE

If we're angry and pouring gasoline on the fire, it can be really difficult to back down and forgive the other person. And if we're also keeping score, our desire is often to get the other person to feel the weight of what they've done to us. But that's the opposite of how God treats us. He extends grace to us, and he instructs us to forgive others as he forgives us through Christ (Eph. 4:32).

A favorite Myers family story illustrates how difficult it can be to give others grace. It's a story Marcia loves to tell.

> MARCIA: I don't really enjoy card games, especially when the whole family is involved. By the end of the game, somebody is always in tears. That's what happened a few years ago when we were playing Uno. Maybe you've played this game. It doesn't involve a lot of strategy. You try to make the other players draw cards

while you try to get rid of yours. And the first person without any cards wins.

Four of us were playing: Kevin, Jake, who was seventeen at the time, Jadon, who was eight, and me. Jadon was getting very close to winning and had just a few cards left. He could hardly contain his excitement. Being the youngest child, he didn't win a lot. So this was a special moment for him, a well-earned check in the win column for all the times his siblings had beaten him at something.

Just before Jadon was able to claim victory, Jake put down a draw-two card, which meant Jadon had to draw two cards. Immediately, Jadon's happiness turned to sorrow. He was on the verge of tears, and it was all he could do to hold them in. And then on Jake's next turn, he gave Jadon another draw two! That was more than Jadon could handle. He had a meltdown of biblical proportions. "It's not fair! I was about to win!" he cried.

Jadon comes by his competitiveness honestly. He's like his dad, if you ask me. Kevin is supercompetitive. That's one of the reasons I don't like to play games. But if I'm honest, I'm kind of competitive too. If I weren't, I wouldn't care if Kevin always won. So there it is. We're both competitive.

As a mom, I wanted to fix the problem. Should I tell Jake, "Go easy on your little brother. Giving him two draw-two cards is a bit much." Or say to Jadon, "C'mon, it's only a game. You're going to have to toughen up if you want to make it in the real world."

What you don't know is that a few turns before Jadon received the two draw-two cards from Jake, he had given Jake not one, not two, not three, but *four* draw-four cards! He had loaded Jake with cards. But at that moment, all Jadon could focus on was that Jake had given him two draw twos in a row just as he was about to win.

The same thing happens in marriage. We keep a record of the wrongs we've suffered, but we fail to remember our own offenses. It's human nature. You've probably had conversations with people who share all the ways their spouse has dealt them a draw-two card. They cite every detail of the offense. They pour out their sorrow, bitterness, and anger about the way they've been wronged. And their complaints seem legitimate. But then you later learn the rest of the story. It may take weeks, even years, but you eventually find out about all the draw fours they've dealt their spouse.

If we want our marriages to experience the Second Happy, we need to recognize our own faults and stop keeping score. We have to put down the gasoline bucket of self-justification and pick up the water bucket of grace. We need to forgive.

> To experience the Second Happy, we need to recognize our own faults and stop keeping score.

One of the best ways to do that is to cultivate a spirit of gratitude. How many people do you know who feel grateful and angry at the same time? If you regularly thank God for his grace to you and for your spouse and the kind things they do, you will find it easier to pick up the water bucket.

3. RESTORE THE RELATIONSHIP

Marcia and I learned the lesson of the two buckets many years ago, and we consistently followed the practice of using the water bucket to put out our fires and forgive each other. It has become a consistent part of our lives, not only with each other but with our children and people outside our family. But it wasn't until recently that God pressed on me that there was another part of the practice I needed to embrace and make a part of my life.

As I've previously mentioned, my parents divorced when I was in middle school. After the divorce, Dad proved to be less and less the Christian he claimed to be. He also became so consumed with his own life that, for all practical purposes, he discarded me. My two brothers eventually went to live with him, and my younger sister became the pawn he used to get under Mom's skin. Meanwhile I was completely ignored.

Because of my dad's actions, I ended my relationship with him and never asked him for anything after I turned seventeen. He remained out of my life. By the time I was twenty-five, I was married, settled a thousand miles away from Michigan in Georgia, and leading 12Stone Church. All four of our children were born here. Today, they range in age from thirty-one to sixteen. Two are married, and between them, we have three grandbabies who are awesome! In all those years, our kids never knew their grandfather. They only knew he lived in Michigan. My dad chose to be a poor father to me, and he chose not to be a part of our lives. He and I were estranged for almost forty years.

In September 2018, I was doing a teaching series at the church, and for one part of it I interviewed Jeff Foxworthy. I've always enjoyed his "you might be a redneck" humor, but this interview went beyond his comedy and into his past. Jeff spoke about how his dad had failed as a father and had disappeared from his family. But years later, when Jeff came to faith, he worked to restore that relationship.

Jeff didn't know it, but I was dumbfounded by his ability to reconcile with his dad. After the interview I asked him, "Why and how did you do that?"

"Well," he said, "it was less about my dad and more about me. I needed to let it go, inside me. So, since I was freed up in God, I was able to forgive and be restored with my dad. After all, I only have one dad on earth. But it was more about me settling it and less about my dad solving it."

I understood the need to forgive. And I had forgiven my dad years before. But I could not get my head around having any kind of relationship with him.

I didn't think anything more about it—until a couple of months later, during a prayer time. For some months I had been praying, "Heavenly Father, I want more of you." It was a simple and sincere prayer. But on this particular day, the Lord spoke back to me into my spirit: *Kevin, if you want more of me, you have to be more like me.*

"Lord, how am I not like you?" I asked.

You forgive, but you do not restore. I do, but you do not.

Of course, I argued with God. I made a list of all the people I remembered having forgiven and restored in relationships. Then God spoke three names to me. And I couldn't argue with him anymore.

"You're right, God. I do not forgive and restore," I prayed. "And I will gladly forgive, but I will not restore."

As you might guess, the first name on the list was my dad's. But there was no way on earth I was going to offer to restore that relationship. I was fifty-seven and he was seventy-seven. I'd been telling stories of our estrangement in the church for thirty years. My kids had forgotten he even existed. And in this season of my life, I needed nothing from my dad and had zero interest in reconnecting with him.

Well, you probably know where this is going next. One of the great things about God is that when you walk with him, he will not let something go when it is his best for your life. And even though I'd never before sensed the Lord making an issue of my estrangement from my dad, he was doing so now. Finally, I gave in and asked my sister for Dad's number. I called him and offered to fly up to Michigan to see him.

In January 2019, I did something I never imagined doing. I had lunch with my dad. And we talked honestly, discussing our forty years of separation. We agreed to forgive each other and restore our relationship. During the conversation, he said he had been praying to God for years that we would be reconciled, but he believed he could not initiate it.

On June 16, 2019, I acknowledged him on Father's Day for the first time in forty years. And the following November, I felt compelled by the Spirit to fly him down to meet the whole family for Thanksgiving. It sort of freaked out my kids. Imagine my adult kids walking into our home and meeting their grandpa for the first time. It was surreal.

Restoring relationships can be painful and horribly difficult. It was for me. I did not want to make that phone call to my dad when

God prompted. However, I truly wanted to be more like my heavenly Father. And for that to happen, I had to reconnect with my earthly father and restore our relationship. That is what God did for us through Christ, and it is what he is asking us to do with one another.

Now, Marcia and I are not trying to minimize or ignore the pain and loss you may have experienced in your marriage. We have our list of things we've needed to forgive, and we're certain you have yours. We also acknowledge that choosing the water bucket isn't always easy. Those steps of putting out the fire, forgiving, and restoring a relationship take work. But it's possible.

You may be thinking either, *You wouldn't forgive and restore her if you were in my shoes. She's caused me too much pain,* or *You don't know what he's done to me!* You're right. We don't. But we can tell you this: if David and Loni Metter were able to use the water bucket to put out the fire, forgive, and restore their marriage, you can too. Why? Because David's ex-wife tried to hire someone to kill him. Their story is so sensational that the Oxygen network show *Murder for Hire* told the tale in an episode titled "Daddy's Girl."

Murder for Hire

When I met David, I connected with him right away. I could tell he was a kindred spirit. He and Loni are sharp. Their marriage is strong, their business is successful, and their pursuit of Jesus is sincere. Marcia and I loved having them as members of our small group. What we did not know was the bitterness they were required to process and how much they had to forgive.

David and Loni have a blended family. If you sat down with them for a heart-to-heart conversation about marriage, Loni would say, "There's a reason why God wants one marriage. You not only bring *your* stuff into a new marriage, but you bring an entire group of people with you and *their* stuff too."

Loni brought her daughter and son plus a history with her ex-husband, who was mostly an absent father, into their marriage. David brought his four girls. They were the only positive outcome of his tumultuous nineteen-year marriage to Chrissy. Their marriage had started out well enough, but Chrissy's continual use of the gasoline bucket to escalate problems, her constant criticism of David, and her inability to cut the cord with her parents made their home toxic. Eventually they divorced, and David moved to Atlanta.

But Chrissy descended into bitterness. She was constantly making trouble, and that followed David into his marriage with Loni. Chrissy was determined to ruin David. She made false accusations of abuse, calling him a wife beater and a child abuser. On several occasions, she called both David's and Loni's employers to slander them. The couple couldn't even walk onto a soccer field to support their children without facing public scorn because of all the lies Chrissy was telling the other parents. She even contacted Loni's ex-husband and tried to convince him to turn on them. According to David, she was like a crab in a bucket. Crabs don't want other crabs to get out, so they use their claws to drag them down to the bottom.

Even though David was a long-distance dad, he made staying connected to his kids a priority. His daughters visited him every summer. But at the end of their visit in the summer of 2010, when they got to the airport to fly back home, David's oldest daughter broke down and refused to get on the plane. She begged her daddy not to make her go back to her mom. David knew that if he didn't send her home, he would be breaking a court order. He also knew that protecting his daughter was more important. So he decided to keep her in Georgia and went to court to gain full custody of her. Later, to rescue his other three girls from that volatile situation, he filed for sole custody of them as well.

That set Chrissy off. She and her dad, Al, met with Patrick, an old friend from high school, and they asked him to find someone to kill David. But instead of planning the murder, Patrick informed the police. As a result, an undercover officer pretended to be a hit man and set up a meeting with them. During their initial conversation, the pretend hit man gave Al every opportunity to back out, but he was emphatic. He said, "He's taken everything. He's taken one girl, and now he wants the other three."

Once the murder was contracted, the police notified David. They asked him to help them stage a photograph as proof of his death, which they doctored to make it look as if he had been shot. When the undercover officer met with Al and Chrissy to show them the photo as confirmation of the murder, they were arrested. Both were tried and convicted, and they're now serving long prison sentences. And David's girls came to live with him.

Choosing the High Road

I think it's fair to say that David and Loni had many legitimate complaints about Chrissy. Having your ex-spouse try to turn the kids against you with vicious lies could easily suck anyone into anger, bitterness, and malice. It would be easy to want to fight fire with fire. And we can't even imagine what it would feel like to have someone plot to have us killed! It certainly would be tempting to pick up the gasoline bucket and use it to hurt that person. But David and Loni never did.

How were they able to keep choosing the water bucket over and over? First, they made Jesus the center of their marriage, unlike in their first marriages. Second, they committed to moving forward together. "We can't go back and fix the pain, shame, and guilt of our past relationships," said David. "But we can replace generational sin with a new legacy of generational love for our new family." To do that, they chose several nonnegotiable values to define their new blended family: commitment with honesty, alignment with unity, and good choices to define quality of life.

Coming into a second marriage, they believed they needed to be completely honest about their past to help cement those values. As they shared, something funny happened. When one confessed something like "When I was in high school, I did this," the other responded, "Oh, yeah, well, when I was in college, I did *this*." They shared every failure and shortcoming they could think of. It felt painful and necessary at the time, but they laugh about it now. They affectionately refer to it as their "one-up" conversation. It was important that they put everything on the table. To this day, they recommend that couples entering a second marriage have this kind of conversation.

The Metters' strategy created a good foundation for handling all their problems, even those as big as the ones they had to face with Chrissy. But they still had to choose to use the water bucket. Both of them can point to a specific moment when they chose forgiveness. Reflecting on all the family moments Chrissy had forfeited because of her bitterness and poor choices, David and Loni felt pity for her. Bitterness or resentment didn't fit into the new legacy they were creating for their blended family. So they decided, "We are done. As God forgives us, we forgive her."

It didn't make Chrissy's actions right or resolve the broken trust she created in the relationship. It simply meant that they accepted the consequences of Chrissy's choices and then chose not to join her in hatred or bitterness. But while David and Loni were willing to restore their relationship with Chrissy, she wasn't. At the hearing to remove Chrissy's parental rights, when she could have expressed regret for her actions, she instead told the court that what she had done was "no big deal" since, after all, "nothing happened."

While restoration has not been possible so far with Chrissy, the story is different with Loni's ex-husband. He recently moved into a house down the street from the Metters, and he is getting to know his children again. Loni's kids are willing to reengage with their father and hope to have a healthy relationship with him. In the spirit of forgiveness and restoration, Loni and David are intentional about including him and his new wife in their family celebrations.

Meanwhile, David and Loni continue to pray for their ex-spouses to find what they have found: faith in Christ as the foundation for peace in their lives. They each went through a marriage that went from happy to unhappy and stayed that way until it ended. But they are determined to make their second marriage work. And with God's help, they've found the Second Happy. They've worked hard to develop a healthy relationship centered on Christ and to live according to God's principles. They make it less about *trying* and more about *doing*. That's one of the reasons Marcia and I fell in love with the Metters. They don't simply talk about having a better marriage. They put God's principles into action with everyone around them. They have made using the water bucket a habit in their lives.

How do you handle the sparks, embers, and flames that pop up in your relationships, particularly the ones with your spouse? You can't keep switching back and forth between the gasoline bucket and the water bucket and expect to experience the Second Happy in your marriage. In fact, that kind of inconsistency will create an *unhappy* undercurrent in your relationship. So choose your bucket wisely.

If you have a background like mine, then you need to let your heavenly Father re-parent you through the power of the Holy Spirit. He can teach you to be quick to listen, slow to speak, and slow to anger. And you can learn to extend grace, just as grace has been given to you by God through Christ. By consistently choosing to pick up the water bucket, you can build a marriage like no other.

CONVERSATION FOR A COUPLE

Answer these questions on your own, with your spouse doing the same. Then make an appointment with each other to discuss your answers. Have an honest conversation with the goal of serving each other in order to develop a better marriage. Be honest with your feelings, but focus on how *you* can change by applying the practice to yourself, not your spouse.

1. How were relational difficulties handled in your family when you were growing up? How much have that modeling and those habits influenced how you respond now?

2. How do you respond when you experience a troubling relational spark, ember, or flame with your spouse or children? How many times out of ten would you say you tend to use the gasoline bucket? Would your spouse agree with your assessment? When you use the gasoline instead of the water bucket, why do you think you do it?

3. How would your relationship change if you learned to use only the water bucket? Are you willing to commit to learn that process and make that change?

4. What help do you need from the Holy Spirit to help you use only the water bucket? In what ways do you need him to re-parent you? What can you do to remind yourself as you grow angry that you need to pick up the water bucket, not the gasoline bucket?

Once you've shared your answers, discuss what each of you needs to do as a result of your conversation.

DISCUSSION FOR A SMALL GROUP

1. If you could go on any kind of vacation to any place in the world, where would you go and why?
2. Was your upbringing more like Kevin's or Marcia's? Explain.
3. What kinds of things tend to set you off or make you angry? Why do they bother you?
4. How would you rate yourself on a scale of 1 to 10, with 1 being "slow to anger" and 10 being "hot-tempered"?
5. How do you think the way you handle anger (based on the rating above) affects your relationship with your spouse? Your family? Your colleagues?
6. What would change in your marriage if you were able to lower your rating down to "slow to anger"?
7. Which practice do you find most difficult to do when conflict arises and why?
   - Pause and put out the fire.
   - Forgive the offense.
   - Restore the relationship.
8. What are you willing to do to become someone who is slow to anger (Prov. 15:18), uses a soft answer to turn away wrath (Prov. 15:1), brings calm (Prov. 29:11), and forgives others (Eph. 4:32)?

Conclusion

God's dream for your marriage is the Second Happy. And he wants it for the marriage you have today. That is his heart for you. The more you invest in your marriage, the better and the happier it will be.

Now you understand the seven practices Marcia and I have learned through nearly forty years of marriage:

1. Break the quit cycle
2. Get your hands up
3. Pick a fair fight
4. Take a knee or two
5. Don't settle for the hollow Easter bunny
6. Evict the elephant
7. Choose your bucket wisely

We are honored to be your coaches. If you have not yet entered into God's Second Happy for your marriage, we encourage you to keep using the seven practices. And keep your hands up. God always wants to help couples with their marriage.

As your marriage grows and becomes more content, pass along

what you've learned to others. Teach them what you've learned. Lead a small group using this book. Share the benefit of your wisdom and encouragement.

One final thought: knowing what to do isn't what makes a marriage happy, but actually doing what you know. Jesus was teaching this concept when he said, "Now that you know these things, you will be blessed if you do them" (John 13:17).

Live the practices consistently, day after day. Doing them to get to the Second Happy is like a renovation. And continuing to do them once your house is already beautiful is how you *remain* happy.

We celebrate your growth,
Kevin and Marcia Myers

Acknowledgments

Kevin and Marcia would like to thank the couples who allowed their stories to be told in this book. Your honesty and openness will help many find the Second Happy in their marriages.

Charlie would like to thank his wife, Stephanie, for editing the manuscript prior to submission, and his daughter Hannah, who served as his editorial assistant during the editing process. You are both awesome!

Notes

INTRODUCTION

1. Kevin Myers with Charlie Wetzel, *Grown-Up Faith: The Big Picture for a Bigger Life* (Nashville: Thomas Nelson, 2018).

PRACTICE 1: BREAK THE QUIT CYCLE

1. Anne and Ray Ortlund, *You Don't Have to Quit: How to Persevere When You Want to Give Up* (Nashville: Thomas Nelson, 1994).
2. John Maxwell, "The View from the Top of the Hill," July 12, 2016, https://www.johnmaxwell.com/blog/the-view-from-the-top-of-the-hill/.
3. Todd Wagner and John McGee, *Re|engage: Reconnect, Reignite, Resurrect* (Dallas: Watermark Church, 2016), 11.

PRACTICE 2: GET YOUR HANDS UP

1. Jerry Seinfeld, *I'm Telling You for the Last Time*, performed live August 9, 1998, New York City (HBO), YouTube video, https://www.youtube.com/watch?v=J020Hmu7P-g.
2. Neil Clarkson, "World Horse Population Likely to Be over 60 Million, Figures Suggest," Horsetalk.co.nz, July 10, 2017, https://www.horsetalk.co.nz/2017/07/10/world-horse-population-60-million/.
3. Kevin A. Myers and John C. Maxwell, *Home Run: Learn God's Game Plan for Life and Leadership* (New York: FaithWords, 2014).

PRACTICE 3: PICK A FAIR FIGHT

1. Tim Adams, "Ultimate Fighting Championship: The Fight of Our Lives?" *The Guardian*, March 26, 2017, https://www.theguardian.com/sport/2017/mar/26/ultimate-fighting-championship-fight-of-our-lives-mma-donald-trump-vladimir-putin-conor-mcregor.
2. David Augsburger, *Sustaining Love: Healing and Growth in the Passages of Marriage* (Ventura, CA: Regal, 1988).

PRACTICE 6: EVICT THE ELEPHANT

1. Francine Rivers, *Redeeming Love* (New York: Bantam, 1991).

PRACTICE 7: CHOOSE YOUR BUCKET WISELY

1. John C. Maxwell, *Developing the Leaders Around You* (Nashville: Thomas Nelson, 1995).
2. James Fisher and Vibhu Talwar, "Man Throws Gasoline on Embers," Fisher and Talwar, February 20, 2013, https://www.fishertalwar.com/man-throws-gasoline-on-embers.
3. "Gasoline Safety," City of Bellingham, Washington, accessed October 8, 2020, https://www.cob.org/services/safety/education/Pages/gasoline.aspx.

About the Authors

KEVIN AND MARCIA MYERS have been married for forty years. They have four children and four grandchildren. Kevin is the founding senior pastor of 12Stone Church, one of the most influential churches in the United States. A gifted communicator, influential leader, and strategic thinker, Kevin planted the church in 1987 and has grown it to eight campuses and a strong online presence. He mentors pastors and church planters, speaks at churches and businesses around the country, and serves on the General Board of the Wesleyan Church as well as the Wesleyan Investment Foundation (WIF), a nonprofit corporation that assists churches with capital needs.

CHARLIE WETZEL is a writer, teacher, and cook. He wrote *The Marvel Studios Story*, the screenplay for the award-winning short film "The Candy Shop," and more than a hundred books with *New York Times* bestselling author John C. Maxwell. When Charlie isn't writing, he's creating cooking videos for his YouTube channel "Becoming a Cook" with Stephanie, his wife of twenty-eight years, or they're spending time with their three adult children.